USK401/89

14⁰⁰
7⁰⁰

CARIBBEAN ADVENTURES

Classic Cajun Cooking and Tales
from the Reign of the Pirates

D1305357

ADLAI HOUSE PUBLISHING
P.O. Box 935
Lakeside, CA 92040

CARIBBEAN ADVENTURES
Classic Cajun Cooking and Tales from the Reign of the Pirates

Copyright © 1994 by Adlai House Publishing

Artwork by Adlai House Publishing

Resident pirate and editor—Ed Landry

Cover illustration of pirate by David Landry

All rights reserved. This book may not be reproduced, in whole or in part, in any form without permission, except for brief book reviews. Inquiries should be addressed to Adlai House Publishing, P.O. Box 935, Lakeside, CA 92040.

First Edition

1 2 3 4 5 6 7 8 9   97 96 95 94

QUANTITY PURCHASES
Certain groups, organizations or clubs may qualify for special rates when ordering quantities of this title. Please send your request on your letterhead stationery to Special Sales, Adlai House Publishing, P.O. Box 935, Lakeside, CA 92040.

ISBN 0-9630244-1-8

Library of Congress Catalog Card Number
94-70556

Printed in the United States of America.

An earth-friendly book.
Printed on recycled paper

CARIBBEAN ADVENTURES

RECIPES

Features and Stories index

The Cajuns

French settlers living in Nova Scotia refused to bow the knee to British rule and left Canada. They sailed south to Louisiana, a land where they could be free of English tyranny. The word "Cajun" was the short version of the harder to pronounce "Arcadian," and the title stuck to the new immigrants. Fishermen, farmers and trappers by trade, the Cajuns fit right in to the easy-going lifestyle of southern Louisiana. Life was in no hurry on the bayou. They liked it that way then, and they still like it that way now.

Once in the new land, the Cajuns soon incorporated the local spices into their own cuisine. They also adopted the spicy Caribbean cooking traditions they learned from the Haitian refugees living in the region. The rich, lavish foods of the wealthy, Creole plantation owners nearby added a spice or two to Cajun kitchens. A new food was born. The smell of gumbos and jambalayas, simmering in giant black iron pots, drifted across the lakes and swamps into New Orleans. Life was enjoyed and their cookouts were an important part of that enjoyment. Their families and friends were as strong as their coffee. Isn't that the way it ought to be?

So what did the Cajuns and the pirates have in common? The answer probably depends on who you ask, but in reality there was only one thing—geography. They shared some of the same space. The pirates for the most part were renegades and deserters from France and England, and some came from Caribbean isles like Jamaica. Many of them used the bayous to hide from the law and as secret burial grounds for ill-gotten treasure.

Both the Cajuns and the pirates left their mark on the Gulf of Mexico. The Cajuns filled the stomachs of the region and the pirates emptied the pockets.

Today, the pirates are gone and the Cajuns are still around and fortunately, for us, so is their cooking. Cajun cooking stands alone. If you haven't tasted it, then you have lived your whole life without having eaten. How did you survive? It is about time you started. This book will give you a chance to redeem yourself.

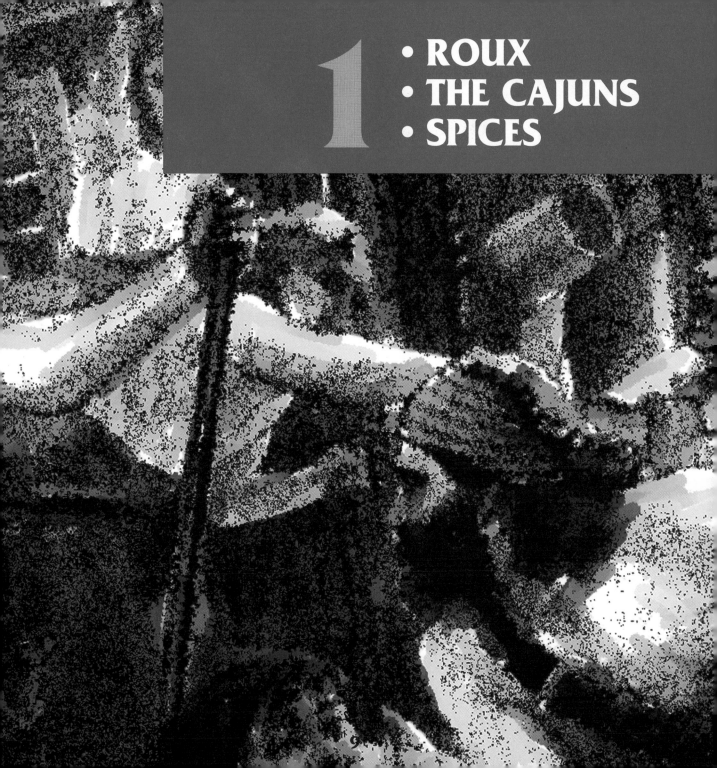

1
- **ROUX**
- **THE CAJUNS**
- **SPICES**

Secrets of the Roux
and Cajun rice too!

Roux (rhymes with stew) is the foundation for most Cajun dishes. It is not difficult to make, but it takes a little patience. There is no secret to making good roux. Once you start cooking it you have to stay with it. Don't leave it unattended. Follow the simple instructions and make sure you don't get the heat too high, and you will get excellent results.

Equipment. Some chefs insist on an iron skillet. You can get good results using any pan. Use a wooden stirring spoon.

Ingredients. Roux is generally prepared in small quantities, but you can make it in larger amounts and refrigerate it. The main ingredients are flour and oil. Animal fat (lard) produces the best flavor, but if you are especially health conscious you may want to use butter, margarine or vegetable oils. White flour is the other component. An equal amount of flour and oil or lard is normally the best. A half cup of roux is made with 1/2 cup of flour

and 1/2 cup oil (not 1/4 plus 1/4). Use this formula to calculate your portions.

Cooking Temperature. The cooking temperature is the single most important variable in the process. Whether cooked over gas or electric, you will need an even medium heat. If the oil is smoking, this is an indication that the temperature is too high and the roux will burn. If you notice black specks in the roux, it is probably burnt and should be discarded. A burnt roux will spoil your Cajun dish.

Preparing the Roux. Melt the oil or fat in a skillet and slowly add the flour, stirring constantly until you have the color roux called for in your recipe. IMPORTANT: Don't increase the heat to produce a darker roux. The roux darkens in color and changes flavor when the cooking time is increased. The temperature is a constant for all colors of roux. Once the temperature is correct, the color is determined by the cooking time. The following guide will give you some idea of what you might expect in preparing your roux:

COLOR OF ROUX	TIME NEEDED	USES
White or light roux	7 minutes	Vegetable sauces and chowder bases
Medium or peanut-colored roux	7-12 minutes	Creoles and game
Dark mahogany roux	12-15 minutes	Preferred in gumbos and bisques

Working with Roux. Depending on the recipe, you will usually be asked to prepare the roux ahead and add the roux to the other ingredients. When adding liquids to the roux, be sure you are using hot liquids and that you stir constantly while adding. The ratio of liquid to roux will determine the thickness of your sauce. This is a matter of personal taste and can be varied by the cook for desired results.

Cajun Rice

There are as many ways to prepare rice as there are cooks preparing rice. If you are skilled at and content with the results you are getting, then don't read any further. If you have tried every method ever devised with unhappy results, buy a rice cooker. They are one of the best investments you can make for your kitchen and sanity.

Rice used in Cajun dishes is light, fluffy rice. Here is a cooking procedure which works quite well. Remember to watch rice carefully since it can be burned. To serve six people with generous portions, use three cups of clean rice. Use a 2-quart or larger pan that has a tight-fitting lid. Rinse the rice with cold water and place it in the pan. Cover with enough water to measure the same height as the rice. Example: If the rice in the pot is 1 1/2 inches high, make sure the water level when added to the rice is 1 1/2 inches above the rice. Add 1/2 teaspoon of salt and bring to a boil, stirring occasionally. Cover, reduce heat to low and cook 15-20 minutes. Do not uncover during cooking. Fluff with fork before serving. If this doesn't work for you, go get that rice cooker.

What the Pirates Really Ate

If we believed Hollywood, we would conclude that the pirates lived the life of a party animal. That would only be half right. It was no party. Long, grueling voyages with little or nothing to show for their suffering was a more common experience. Food supply frequently ran out and crews lived on bread crumbs and rain water for nourishment. Some party!

When they reached land, they raided the hen houses and killed local cattle and then gorged themselves at the landowners' expense. But soon it was back to sea again, fleeing local militia or Spanish warships. Living out of a suitcase is one thing, but this was life out of a rotted larder. Roaches and worms turned their stores of ship grain into slimy masses of grub-infested froth. (We decided not to include this as one of the recipes in this book.) Voyages frequently started out with rum and feast and ended with starvation and death. One miserable rogue described his time at sea this way:

> "All my gums were rotted. They gave out a black and putrid smell. My thighs and lower legs were black and gangrenous. I could not eat. Many of our people died of it every day and we saw bodies thrown into the sea constantly, three or four at a time."

Makes you want to go to sea, doesn't it? Pirates were sometimes as interested in getting food as they were gold when they seized a vessel crossing their path. A typical small merchant vessel crossing the Atlantic carried 4 tons of beef, 1 ton of pork, 100 bushels of various grains and dried vegetables and 10,000 gallons of beer, rum and cider. This presented a mouth-watering prize too tempting to pass up for malnourished crews. It is no wonder that the accounts of pirate attacks describe them as bands of wild animals swarming onto the decks.

Pirates that stayed closer to home in the Caribbean became hunters on their islands and cured their meats by smoking and salting them, but even the best-prepared provisions didn't last long against the elements and rodents when they went to sea.

Even with 25,000 vessels sailing the seas, it was still slim pickings at times for the buccaneers. Crews would go for months without ever sighting another ship. Gambling consumed their seemingly endless days on the deck and in the smelly holds. Mutinies were not that uncommon as discontented crews grew restless. Food shortages only increased the tensions.

It was a life of feast and then famine, but mostly famine. They were criminals on the run, and there were no fast-food restaurants. Except for the few who settled down and enjoyed the cuisine of their countries, most of the cutthroats never tasted shrimp bisque or crawfish gumbo. This cookbook is not about foods the pirates ate. It is about the foods the pirates missed. The finest cuisine on the planet was right under their noses, but they chose to eat sour biscuits and drink bilge water in their pursuit of rainbows and elusive dreams. The lesson the pirates learned too late was, "When you sail across life's seas, be sure and take time to pull into port and taste the gumbo."

DICTIONARY OF CAJUN/CREOLE SPICES AND TERMS

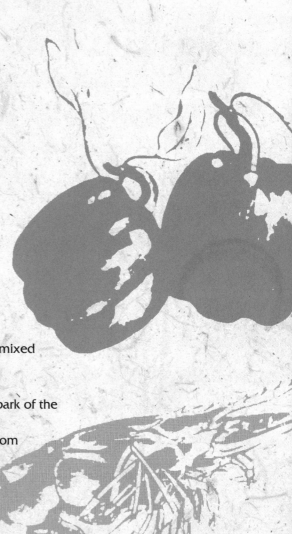

Andouille — Spicy smoked pork sausage.

Basil — Herb native to Europe. Aromatic leaves used for seasoning.

Baste — To pour pan drippings or sauce over meat while cooking.

Bay leaves — Dry aromatic leaf of bay or bayberry is used for seasoning.

Blend — Combine or mix until a consistent uniform mixture is obtained.

Cardamom — Seasoning made from seeds of Asiatic plant.

Cayenne — Condiment made from the pungent fruit of the cayenne red pepper. Not to be confused with the Cajun word for a container, as in "Put dem grits in de cayenne (can), Zeke."

Chicory — Root of this plant is dried, roasted, ground and mixed with coffee.

Chop — To quickly cut into rough pieces.

Cinnamon —An aromatic spice made from dried, ground bark of the cinnamomum tree.

Cloves —East Indian spice used whole or ground. Made from dried flower of tree.

Cracklins — Crisp, browned rind of pork fat after rendering.

Dice — To cut into small, even cubes.

Dissolve — Cause to turn into liquid form either by adding to another liquid or by heating.

Filé — Powder from ground sassafras root and used to flavor and thicken gumbos. (No substitutes on this one, folks.)

Dictionary continued . . .

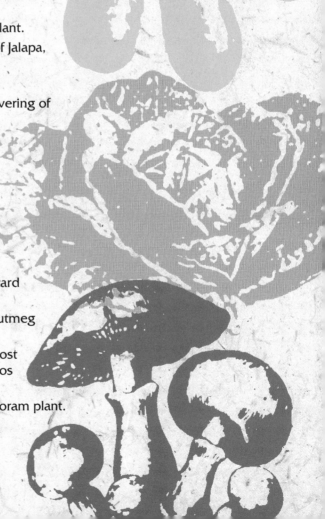

Garlic — Bulb with strong, distinct odor and flavor. Divisions of the bulb are called cloves.

Garnish — To decorate.

Ginger — Spice made from dried, ground root of tropical Asian plant.

Grind — To crush or break apart by mechanical means.

Grits — Coarse ground corn or grain. Cooked like a firm porridge and served as a side dish.

Head Cheese — Jellied loaf or sausage containing chopped, boiled, seasoned meat from the head, feet, heart and tongue.

Horseradish — Shredded or grated root of a Lapathifolia plant.

Jalapeño — Hot red or green peppers named for the city of Jalapa, Mexico.

Knead — Press, fold and stretch dough with hands.

Mace — Aromatic spice made from dried yellow or red covering of the nutmeg kernel. Not to be confused with the Cajun term for a young lady, as in, "Mace, Ak lak yore raid dreyess."

Marinade — Seasoned sauce for soaking meat or fish before cooking.

Marinate — To soak meat or fish in seasoned sauce before cooking.

Mince — Cut or chop into very small pieces.

Molasses — Syrup produced in refining sugar.

Mustard — Condiment made from mixing powdered mustard seeds with wine, vinegar or water and spices.

Nutmeg — Spice made by grating or grinding seed from nutmeg tree.

Okra — Long edible pod from tropical plant. One of the most important flavoring and thickening ingredients in gumbos and soups.

Oregano — Herb made from dried leaves of a type of marjoram plant.

15

Dictionary continued . . .

Paprika — Mild, powdered seasoning made from sweet red peppers.

Parsley — Herb with lacy leaves used to garnish and season food.

Pepper — Spice made from dried black fruit of vine from East Indies.

Pimiento — Mild red pepper used for seasoning and as a stuffing for green olives.

Roux — Thickening and flavoring agent made by cooking equal amounts of oil and flour until desired color and flavor is achieved.

Sage — Herb made from aromatic grey-green leaves of sage shrub.

Sauté — Quickly fry meat or vegetables in small amount of oil, stirring continually.

Sesame oil — Oil derived from seed of plant from tropical Asia.

Simmer — To cook gently just below boiling point.

Soy Sauce — Salty, brown liquid made by fermenting soybeans in brine.

Steam — Cook something using steam from small amount of boiling water.

Stock — Broth from boiled meat or fish used as base for soups, gravy or sauces.

Tabasco — Trademark name for pungent sauce made from hot peppers.

Thyme — Herb made from leaves of Thymus plant.

V8 — Trademark name for juice made by blending eight varieties of vegetables.

Vanilla — Flavoring extract made from vanilla bean.

Vinegar — Condiment made by fermenting acetic acid beyond the alcohol stage.

Worcestershire — Sauce made of soy, vinegar and spices. First made in Worcester, England.

Conversion Table

LIQUID MEASURE TO MILLILITERS

1/4 teaspoon	1.25 ml
1/2 teaspoon	2.50 ml
3/4 teaspoon	3.75 ml
1 teaspoon	5.00 ml

LIQUID MEASURE TO LITERS

1/4 cup	0.06 Liter
1/2 cup	0.12 Liter
3/4 cup	0.18 Liter
1 cup	0.24 Liter

FAHRENHEIT TO CELSIUS

200-205	95
220-225	105
245-250	120
275-280	135
300-305	150
325-330	165
345-350	175
370-375	190
400-405	205
425-430	220
445-450	230
470-475	245
495-500	260

IF YOU KNOW	AND YOU WANT	MULTIPLY BY
teaspoons	milliliters	5.0
tablespoons	milliliters	15.0
fluid ounces	milliliters	30.0
ounces	grams	28.0
pounds	kilograms	.45
quarts	liters	.95
cups	liters	.24

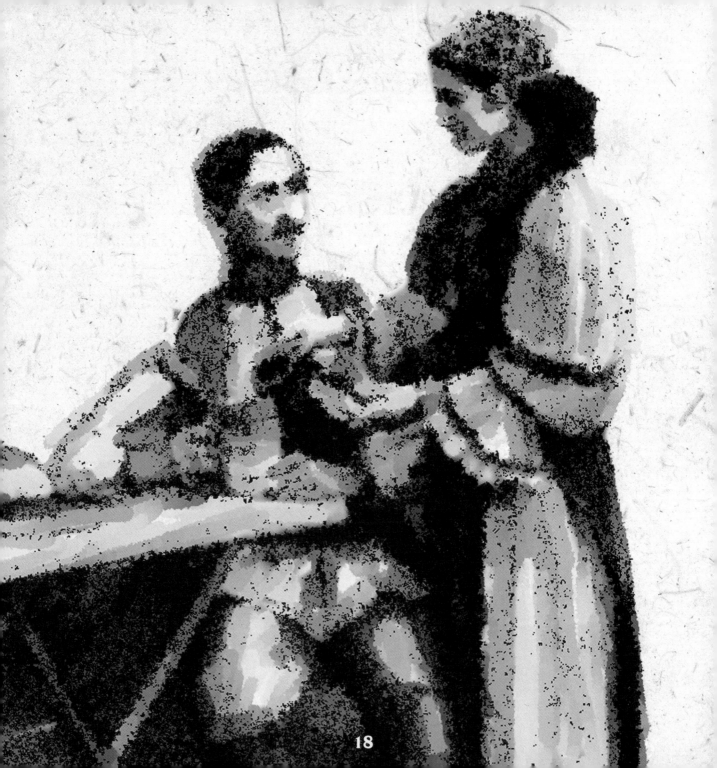

2 APPETIZERS

Disaster in the Winds

From 1565 to 1815 the famous Manila Galleons traveled the Pacific Ocean transporting vast caches of exotic wealth between the Orient and Mexico. The overloaded and unprotected Spanish vessels were an open invitation to anyone who wanted to share in the riches.

The Manila Galleons

The Renaissance had awakened a continent to the arts and finer things. Opportunities were as abundant as dreams. New lands begged to be explored, and the golden coasts of South America and the Caribbean were the reward awaiting the first to conquer them.

Spain was determined to win the prize. Her superior and vast merchant fleet and militia soon established her as the primary player in the competition. Spanish galleons transported billions of dollars in gold and articles of trade back and forth across the Atlantic route.

Even though the English and French were late entries into the race, they had no plans of coming in second or third. The New World belonged to the victor. Some wanted it so badly that they would kill anyone to get it. The only flag they knew was the Jolly Roger.

Golden Highway of the Spanish Galleons

Slave Trade Route

South America and Mexico provided the gold and silver. The Caribbean had the plantations, the ports and the rum. The Gulf and Atlantic states had molasses and cotton and Africa had the cheap labor. Everyone had something someone else wanted. Success was just a matter of putting it all together. There should have been enough land and wealth for everyone, but one thing stood in the way.

APPETIZERS

GALLEY FIRE HOT PEPPER TOAST

1 loaf French bread sliced 1/2 inch thick
1 cup melted butter
1/2 cup finely minced onion

2 teaspoons Tabasco or 1 teaspoon cayenne
pepper
1/2 teaspoon salt

Dip or brush bread slices with mixture. Place on cookie sheet and toast till golden brown. Turn to toast second side if you want them nice and crisp.

SPICY CHEESE FONDUE

1 1/2 pounds grated cheese of your choice
2 cups milk
3 tablespoons butter
3 tablespoons flour
1/4 teaspoon salt

1/4 teaspoon white pepper
1 teaspoon red pepper
1/4 teaspoon dry mustard
1 loaf French bread cubed
fondue pot

Melt butter on medium heat. Add flour, stirring constantly. Do not burn. When a paste forms, slowly add milk, stirring until it becomes thick and creamy. Add cheese and spices and stir until it is melted and smooth. Transfer to fondue pot and serve with French bread cubes and meatballs. Bread cubes can be toasted before serving.

APPETIZERS

CAJUN CHICKEN WINGS

3 pounds chicken wings
Sauce:
  1/4 cup water
  1/2 cup sesame oil
  1/2 cup soy sauce
  1/2 cup brown sugar or molasses
  2 crushed garlic cloves

1 teaspoon salt
1 teaspoon white pepper
1 teaspoon red pepper
1 tablespoon lemon juice
(spices can be increased or hot peppers added
if you are brave)

Marinate overnight or at least for four hours. Spread on a cookie sheet and bake at 350° for 1/2 hour, turning to cook evenly. Baste often. They can be Bar-B-Q'd also.

PIECES OF EIGHT CHEESE CRACKERS

1 cup butter
1/2 teaspoon salt
1/2 to 1 teaspoon cayenne pepper
1 cup grated sharp cheddar cheese

1/4 cup parmesan cheese
1 1/2 cups flour
1 teaspoon baking powder

Cream first 5 ingredients together. Add one teaspoon baking powder to 1 1/2 cups flour and fold into cheese mixture. Turn onto floured board and roll dough to 1/8 inch thick. Cut into 1 1/2 inch circles (or choose whatever shapes suit you). Prick with a fork. Bake in preheated oven at 325° for 10 minutes or until crisp. Serve when cool with your favorite dip or soup.

APPETIZERS

MEATBALLS

3/4 pound ground beef
3/4 pound ground pork
1 medium onion chopped fine
2 crushed garlic cloves
1/2 cup grated parmesan cheese
1 teaspoon oregano
1 tablespoon parsley

2 beaten eggs
1 teaspoon salt
1/2 teaspoon ground black pepper
cayenne pepper to suit taste
1/2 cup dried bread crumbs or cracker crumbs.
   Leftover hushpuppies may also be used.

Mix all ingredients. Form into balls using one tablespoon of mixture each. Pan fry for 10-15 minutes, turning to keep from burning. Serve with toothpicks and Spicy Cheese Fondue.

GATOR TATERS

6 large baking potatoes
1/2 pound bacon or chopped ham
1 cup chopped green onion
2 cups sour cream
1 cup grated cheddar cheese

1/2 cup butter
1/2 teaspoon salt
1/4 teaspoon white pepper
1 teaspoon Worcestershire sauce
parmesan cheese

Clean potatoes and bake at 350° for one hour. Fry bacon, drain and then crumble. Cut baked and cooled potatoes in half. Scoop potato from skins. Set skins on baking sheet. In a large bowl combine potatoes, bacon, onions, sour cream, cheese, butter and seasonings. Mix well until smooth. If it is too stiff, add one or two tablespoons of milk. Spoon mixture back into potato skins. Sprinkle with parmesan cheese. Place under broiler 10 minutes.

The Bored and Bitter Pirate

He had become an American hero. After bravely fighting and helping defeat the British in New Orleans, this member of Jean Lafitte's infamous patriot pirates decided he would take up the domestic life.

Known as Billy "Bowlegs" to his former partners in crime, he became Billy the plantation owner and model citizen. Could a man go from the high adventure of plundering Spanish vessels and fencing illegal slaves to the role of husband of an Indian wife and father to six children? Sure a man could–but not this man. Old Bowlegs got bored and packed his dufflebag. It was back to the sea again.

Kissing his wife and kids goodbye, he chased after his dream. Before long, Billy had formed a colony of fellow adventure-seekers near Pensacola, Florida, and led numerous attacks on merchant and military vessels in Caribbean waters. He buried stashes of gold and silver in the bayous and sounds of Florida.

One day Billy picked on someone bigger than himself. An English warship gave chase and overpowered the pirate vessel. Bowlegs and his crew sped into a shallow harbor, scuttled their ship, and as it sank, swam for shore. Billy decided it had been a long time since he had seen the wife and kids, and so he became "plantation Billy" once again. The defeat and loss of his ship, however, was more than our bowlegged friend could handle. He packed up his family and moved them

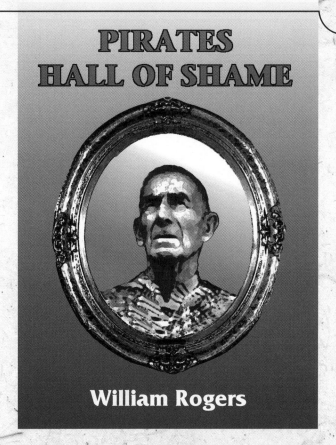

PIRATES HALL OF SHAME

William Rogers

to a small cabin overlooking the harbor where his ship went down.

Failing to salvage his lost treasure, Billy Rogers spent the rest of his miserable years staring, like a junk yard watchdog, at the sea that had defeated him. He never returned to any of his numerous stashes of treasure with their unclaimed promise of riches, but spent the rest of his bitter years brooding over the one that got away. He died at age 95!

3 SALADS

Even the thought of one's crew staging a revolt and commandeering the ship was enough to "shiver the timbers" of the strongest captain. There were compelling reasons crews wanted a change of leadership in the early days of the sail. Long, difficult voyages broke the spirits of many, pointing blame to the one in charge. Disease, starvation and abusive treatment drove some men to desperate measures. A man on death row has little to lose. Many a pirate began his illustrious career with a mutiny, and some of them ended their career the same way. Their feet were always on slippery places.

The most famous of all mutinies was the one which befell the English vessel, *Bounty*, on April 28, 1789. It all began because of breadfruit. England decided they needed a source of food to plant in the West Indies to feed the growing number of slaves. An expedition was sent to Tahiti to investigate the growing process and transport breadfruit plants to the Caribbean. After six months in Tahiti, the *Bounty* set out for the next phase of its expedition. The crew had different ideas. Under the lead of Fletcher Christian, they took over the ship and set Captain William Bligh and seventeen others adrift in a 23-foot launch to die in the South Pacific. With a new sense of freedom the remaining crew returned to Tahiti. Sixteen of the crew decided that would be home for them. The others took twelve women and six native men and sailed on, settling on Pitcairn Island where they burned the Bounty. And they lived happily ever after. Well, not quite.

It seems that the man they had left to die had actually survived the most unbelievable ordeal. By demanding strong loyalty to his every command, Captain Bligh rationed the little water left on the small boat and guided the overloaded rowboat through treacherous shoals and open sea for 41 miserable days. Living on the entrails of seabirds and a few ounces of water a day, the captain with only his limited knowledge of the South Pacific and the tenacity of an angry bulldog managed to avoid hostile islands and navigate the starving, weak crew 3,600 miles to the Island of Timor. It is a feat unequalled to this day. He returned to England and told his story. The lawless crew was hunted by the Crown, and the Tahiti team was captured. Meanwhile, Fletcher Christian had come into a few problems of his own on Pitcairn. It seems the mutiny-bent group still had an authority problem and the island had to be divided up so each could

be his own boss. The natives on the island weren't consulted, and great bitterness resulted. Blood feuds developed, and after ten years only one of the men was still alive. Fletcher Christian had been shot working in his field. Ah, the joys of paradise.

A strange twist to the the whole story is that Captain Bligh went back to gathering breadfruit to take to the West Indies. And being a man who didn't give up, he finally achieved his life's goal. The slaves got their breadfruit. Only one snag. Nobody liked the stuff. They liked Cajun food!

Mutiny!

SALADS

CREOLE COLE SLAW

1 large cabbage
1 green bell pepper
1 teaspoon salt
1/4 teaspoon white pepper

1/2 cup mayonnaise
2 tablespoons sugar
1/4 cup vinegar

Shred cabbage. Cut bell pepper into fine strips. Mix salt, pepper, mayonnaise, sugar and vinegar. Toss bell pepper and cabbage with dressing till well coated. Refrigerate for one hour before serving. Serves six.

SHRIMP SALAD

2 cups shrimp
1 cup chopped celery
2 cups fresh alfalfa sprouts
1/4 cup chopped black olives
1/2 cup mayonnaise
1/4 cup vinegar

1 tablespoon basil
1/2 teaspoon Tabasco
1/2 teaspoon white pepper
1/2 teaspoon salt
lettuce leaves

Clean and cook shrimp. Set aside to cool. Mix all other ingredients in bowl. Fold shrimp in when cool. Serve on lettuce leaves. Serves four to six.

SALADS

ARCADIA BEAN SALAD

1/2 pound bacon
4 cups French cut green beans
2 cups wax beans
1/4 cup salad oil
1/2 cup vinegar

1/2 teaspoon salt
1/4 teaspoon pepper
lettuce leaves
1 can Durkee fried onions

Fry bacon, drain and crumble. Cook, drain and cool beans. Combine oil, vinegar, salt and pepper. Pour over beans. Refrigerate for 1/2 hour. Serve beans on lettuce leaves. Garnish with bacon and fried onions. Serves six.

FRUIT SALAD

one 6 oz package strawberry jello
2 cups fruit juice and/or water
1/2 cup mayonnaise
1 cup cottage cheese

2 cups fresh or frozen strawberries
1 can mandarin oranges
1 can crushed pineapple
1 cup chopped pecans

Drain juice from canned fruit. Add water to make 2 cups. Bring to boil. Dissolve jello in hot juice. Set aside to cool. Blend mayonnaise and cottage cheese together. Add cooled gelatin, fruits and nuts. Pour into mold. Chill until set before serving. Serves six to eight.

SALADS

GREEN AND WHITE SALAD

1 head broccoli
1 head cauliflower
1 package frozen peas
1 cup chopped green onions
1 cup monterey jack or white cheddar cheese
   diced into very small cubes

Dressing:
   1 cup sour cream
   1 cup mayonnaise
   1/2 teaspoon salt
   1/2 teaspoon white pepper
   2 tablespoons vinegar
   1/4 teaspoon cayenne pepper

Clean and cut broccoli and cauliflower using only small bite-size flowerets. Combine with peas, onions and cheese cubes. Pour dressing over salad. Cover and chill for one hour. Serves 10.

CAJUN DEVILED EGGS

12 large eggs
2 tablespoons Dijon mustard
1/4 cup mayonnaise
1/2 cup sour cream
1/2 teaspoon salt

1/2 teaspoon Tabasco
1/4 cup minced, stuffed green olives
paprika
sprigs parsley

Bring two quarts of salted water to a rolling boil. Gently put eggs into boiling water and boil for 10 minutes. Extract eggs. Plunge hot eggs into icy cold water. When eggs have completely cooled, peel eggs and slice in half lengthwise. Scoop egg yellows into a two quart bowl. Set whites on a large platter. Add all ingredients to egg yolks and mix until smooth. Using a tablespoon, fill egg white cavities with yolk mix. Garnish with paprika and parsley. Chill before serving.

Sinking the Wrong Ships

ngland had declared open season on all its enemies, giving great bonuses and recognition to those who sank the most enemy ships. Spain was a prime target, and Portugal was a close second. The problem was that in the early 1700's alliances and treaties changed so frequently that a privateer could attack an enemy one day, and the next day it would be attacking an ally. This fate befell one unfortunate soul named Jack Quelch.

Quelch was on a privateering vessel, the Charles, when a mutiny took place. Captain Plowman was killed and thrown overboard. Jack Quelch was elected as the new captain. The ship initially was to hunt French merchant vessels but Jack Quelch wanted to go after the Portuguese, so a new course to South America was charted.

What Jack Quelch never knew was that during his fateful voyage the English had made peace with the Portuguese. The zealous captain devastated the Portuguese merchant marine by robbing many vessels and sinking nine. Having completed what he thought was a successful privateering mission for his country, he proudly returned to home port in Marblehead, Massachusetts. His crew spread the stories of their exploits all over the town taverns and proudly displayed their trophies. Instead of hearing praise, Jack was shocked to be arrested for piracy. Despite his protests of innocence, Jack Quelch was convicted and hung from the gallows.

Jack Quelch

His crew later admitted that they had kept much of the loot for themselves and that it was buried on the Island of Shoals off New Hampshire. As so often happened, they never had a chance to tell where because they too ended up in a hangman's noose. So what happened to the treasure? No one knows, but the next time you vacation in New Hampshire, you might want to take along a shovel.

4 • SOUPS
• GUMBOS

Ships and Galleons

Jt was truly the golden age of the sail. From the renaissance to the 19th century, ship-building had grown into one of the world's greatest industries. Fueled by rumors of great riches in a New World and the sense of urgency to be the first one to get their hands on it, the European nations entered into a feverish race to get "there" before anyone else. And if they couldn't get there first, they could always take it away from the one who did.

Ships became the key that could unlock a treasure chest full of mystery, wealth and power awaiting the one to risk the treacherous ocean and seize the prize. It was a good time to invest in the shipbuilding industry. The greatest quest of all time was under way and the pace was feverish. Spain soon took the lead, and the others were forced to play catch-up. England wasn't about to come in second, and neither was France or

Portugal. It was the first seagoing olympics, and everyone wanted the gold. Who would win? Whoever had the most and the best ships. By the 1600's more than 25,000 ships were competing in the trade routes.

There was one other entry in the contest, an unofficial registrant. This one didn't care about the rules. The pirates wanted to capture the gold too, but they had a simpler strategy. First, they would steal the ships and then steal the gold. They would just let the others find it, and then they would stake their claim with cannons, muskets and sabers. It proved to be a very persuasive method.

All across Europe shipbuilders designed and crafted their masterpieces of wood, iron and canvas. Kings and queens proudly launched their fleets as patriotic crowds cheered their heros. Colonies in the New World began to spring up, and the flow of gold and silver soon fueled even greater shipbuilding enterprises. Thousands upon thousands of vessels jammed the sea lanes and claimed the trade winds as their own. The cities of the New World began to speak Spanish, English, French, Dutch and Portuguese. Fleets of galleons, barks, warships and merchant vessels flew their country's flags. Well, not all of them did. There were some galleons and warships that hoisted a different flag, one flaunting a skull and crossed bones.

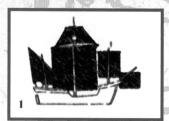

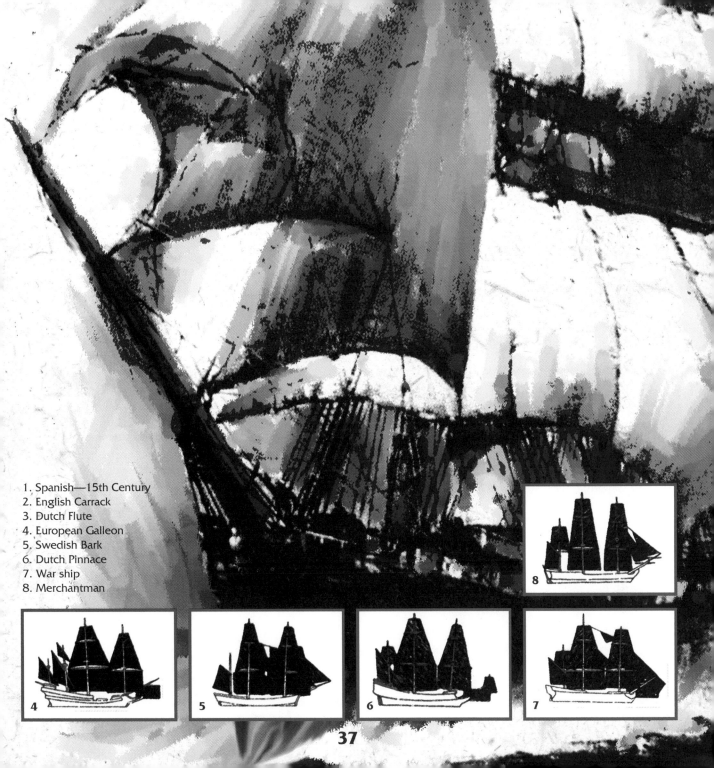

1. Spanish—15th Century
2. English Carrack
3. Dutch Flute
4. European Galleon
5. Swedish Bark
6. Dutch Pinnace
7. War ship
8. Merchantman

SOUPS AND GUMBOS

OYSTER SOUP

1/2 cup light roux
1/4 cup butter
1/2 cup chopped onion
1/2 cup chopped celery
4 cups milk (hot, not scalded)

1 teaspoon salt
1/2 teaspoon white pepper
1/2 cup minced mushrooms
3 dozen small clean oysters and liquid
1/2 cup chopped green onions

Prepare roux (see page 10). Saute onion and celery in butter. Add roux, hot milk and spices. Simmer slowly for 20 minutes stirring occasionally. Add mushrooms, oysters and liquid. Simmer for an additional five minutes. Garnish with green onions and serve with Gally Fire Hot Pepper Toast and a green salad. Serves four.

RED BEAN SOUP

1 pound dried red kidney beans
2 cups chopped onions
1 cup chopped celery
1 cup chopped green pepper
1 pound can cooked tomatoes

3 crushed garlic cloves
2 ham hocks or 2 cups leftover ham pieces.
1 teaspoon salt
1/2 teaspoon black pepper
1 teaspoon Tabasco (if desired)

Wash and soak beans overnight. In the morning cover beans with fresh water. Add onions, celery, green pepper, tomatoes, garlic, ham, spices and Tabasco. Cook until beans are very soft. Serve with Cracklin' Corn Bread. Serves eight.

SOUPS AND GUMBOS

FISH CHOWDER

1/4 cup light roux
1/4 cup oil or butter
1/2 cup chopped onions
1/2 cup chopped celery
1/2 cup chopped green bell pepper
1 minced garlic clove
1 pound can cooked tomatoes
4 cups hot water
4 cups diced potatoes

1/4 teaspoon thyme
1/4 teaspoon oregano
2 bay leaves
1 teaspoon salt
1/2 teaspoon black pepper
1/4 teaspoon red pepper
2 pounds firm, light-fleshed fish cut into 1 inch chunks

Prepare roux (see page 10). Sauté vegetables in oil. Add tomatoes, potatoes, water and roux. Simmer 1/2 hour. Add fish and spices. Cook for an additional 10 minutes before serving with Hushpuppies and Fruit Crush. Serves 8-10.

ANNA'S HERBAL GUMBO

1 bunch each or one 10-ounce package frozen:
  spinach
  turnip greens
  beet tops
  chard
  mustard greens
  1 small cabbage (cut in wedges)
  green onions

4 cups water (vegetable stock)
1/2 cup dark roux
1/4 cup oil or butter
1 pound diced ham
1 cup chopped onion
1 teaspoon salt
1/2 teaspoon black pepper
filé powder to taste

Cook vegetables in four cups of water for 1/2 hour. Prepare roux (see page 10). Strain vegetables and reserve water. In food processor or blender chop vegetables very fine. Sauté ham and onion in oil or butter until onion is soft. Combine vegetables, stock, meat, spices and roux. Simmer for one hour before serving over rice. Serves 4-6.

HAM AND SPLIT PEA SOUP

2 cups dried split peas
6 cups water
1 teaspoon salt
1/2 teaspoon black pepper

1 cup minced onion
1/2 cup chopped celery (leafy tops)
2 cups diced ham
1/2 cup light roux

Wash and soak peas overnight in water. Prepare roux in morning (see page 10). Rinse and cook peas in six cups of water with salt, pepper, onion, celery and ham until peas are soft. Continue to simmer and blend in as much roux as gives desired thickness. Garnish with croutons. Serves six to eight.

CRAB AND GREENS SOUP

2 tablespoons oil or butter
1/2 cup chopped onions
2 minced garlic cloves
1/2 cup chopped celery
2 cups each of chard, cabbage and spinach sliced
   in thin strips

3 cups hot chicken stock
1/2 cup coconut milk (canned or fresh)
1 teaspoon salt
1 tablespoon finely minced jalapeño pepper
2 cups cleaned crab meat

Saute onions, garlic, and celery in butter. Add greens and sauté until limp. Add hot chicken stock, coconut milk, salt and pepper. Simmer for 30 minutes. Add crab. Increase heat and bring to a boil before serving with French bread. Serves four to six.

CAJUN CORN AND SHRIMP SOUP

4 cups of stock (prepare ahead by boiling shrimp
  shells in 4 cups water for 30 minutes. Strain
  and set aside until ready to use)
1/2 cup oil or butter
1 cup chopped bell peppers
2 cups chopped celery
1 cup chopped onion
3 medium tomatoes cut small
1/2 teaspoon salt
1/4 teaspoon black pepper

1/4 teaspoon red pepper
4 cups corn (fresh cut from cob or frozen)
1 16 oz can evaporated milk
2 cups diced, pre-cooked drained potatoes
2 pounds peeled, de-veined shrimp

To liven up flavor choose:
1/4 cup diced jalapiño peppers or,
1/4 cup diced pimientos
Tabasco sauce to your liking

Prepare soup stock. Sauté bell pepper, onion and celery in oil until soft. Add tomatoes, soup stock, seasoning (adjust to your taste), corn and evaporated milk. Simmer slowly for one hour. Add potatoes and simmer another 15 minutes before adding shrimp and your choice of jalapiños, pimientos or Tabasco. Cook only until shrimp turns pink. Serve with *Pieces of Eight* crackers). Serves eight.

CHICKEN AND SAUSAGE GUMBO

3 pounds cut chicken
1/2 cup medium-dark roux
1 cup chopped bell pepper
1/4 cup oil or butter
1 cup chopped onion
1 cup chopped celery
2 cloves garlic minced
1 pound can chopped, peeled tomatoes

2 cups prepared okra (pre-cooked)
1 pound spicy Louisiana sausage
2 bay leaves
1 teaspoon thyme
1/2 teaspoon red pepper
1/2 teaspoon black pepper
1/2 teaspoons salt
Filé gumbo

Cook chicken in 4 cups of water for one hour. Strain stock and set aside. De-bone chicken. Set meat aside. Prepare roux (see page 10), while chicken cooks. Sauté bell pepper, onions, celery and garlic. Add to the roux. Add tomatoes and okra. Simmer 10 minutes. Add sausage, bay leaves, thyme, red and black peppers, salt and chicken stock. Simmer one hour stirring occasionally. Prepare rice while gumbo simmers. Add chicken and simmer 10 minutes more before serving over rice. Sprinkle with filé gumbo to suit individual taste. Serves 10 people or 4 pirates.

SOUPS AND GUMBOS

WEST INDIES SEAFOOD GUMBO

1/2 cup dark mahogany roux
2 pounds medium shrimp
1 pound white crab meat
1 pound crab fingers
1 pint oysters with liquid
1/4 cup oil or butter
2 cups chopped onions
1 cup chopped bell pepper
1 cup chopped celery

2 garlic cloves minced
1 pound prepared okra (pre-cooked)
1 pound can chopped, peeled tomatoes
1 teaspoon salt
1/2 teaspoon black pepper
1/2 teaspoon red pepper
1/2 teaspoon Tabasco
3 bay leaves
1/2 cup chopped green onions

Prepare a dark roux (see page 10) and set aside. Peel shrimp. Boil shells in six cups water for 30 minutes. Strain stock and set aside. Sauté onions, garlic, bell pepper and celery in 1/4 cup oil. Add okra and tomatoes. Simmer 10 min. Add hot shrimp stock to the roux. Mix well, add vegetables and simmer for 20 minutes. Prepare rice (see page 11). Add shrimp and crab to vegetable mixture. Season with salt, peppers, Tabasco and bay leaves. Simmer 15 minutes before adding oysters and liquid. Simmer 10 minutes more. Serve over rice. Garnish with green onions. Serves 12.

FRENCH QUARTER ONION SOUP

1/2 cup dark mahogany roux (see page 10)
4 large onions – sliced thin
1/4 cup butter
2 cups beef broth (can use 2 cubes beef bullion)
4 cups water
1 teaspoon salt

1 teaspoon Tabasco sauce
1 teaspoon Worcestershire sauce
1 tablespoon soy sauce
1 loaf French bread sliced 1" thick and toasted
8 oz Mozzarella cheese, grated

Prepare a dark roux (see page 10). Gradually add roux to hot beef broth. Add 4 cups of water. Bring mixture to a boil. Sauté thinly sliced onions in 1/4 cup butter until tender. Add onions and seasonings to soup. Cover and simmer for 30 minutes. Pour soup into six oven-proof soup bowls and place one slice of toasted French bread on top of each. Cover bread with grated cheese and heat under broiler until cheese is bubbling. Serves six.

A Fellowship of Evil

Pierre La Grand

Adventure was in the wind, and many journeyed to the New World to find it. They weren't all nice people.

One such group roamed the waters of Central America.

Initially known as "Filibusteros" or "Freebooters," they earned an evil reputation. Their life's purpose seemed to be to pillage the Pacific coast of Central America. Eventually they became an organized band called the "Brothers of the Coast." Marauding gangs of up to 500 "Brothers" terrorized villages and vessels. They boarded victims' ships from small boats with knives in their mouths, flintlocks blasting and axes swinging. Their screams terrorized even the bravest opponents. Entire crews were slaughtered or thrown overboard. The Filibusteros' reign of piracy lasted almost 300 years.

Pierre LaGrand became one of the most notorious of the group. He grew up in poverty on the island of Tortuga and later became a leader of the Freebooters. One time he deliberately bored holes in the bottom of his own ship during a battle with a Spanish galleon. He wanted his crew to become desperate so they would fight harder. It worked. LaGrand's success as a pirate inspired many to the same life. His pirates often dressed in fine clothes and fancy silks they had stolen from merchant vessels. Pierre wore a plumed hat like a French gentleman, but his actions were still those of a rogue.

In one unforgettable trek across the Isthmus of Panama, the Brothers of the Coast were carrying great amounts of loot while pursued by the avenging armies. Tired and starving from the long cross-country journey they commandeered small boats and attempted to navigate the treacherous Coco River to get to the Caribbean. Many drowned on its' white waters, and more than 100 million dollars in gold and jewels were strewn along and under the Coco River never to be recovered.

5 · VEGETABLES

Gold Doubloon

Half Doubloon

Quarter Doubloon

Half Doubloon

Early
Gold Doubloon

PIECES OF EIGHT

4 Bits

8 Bits

2 Bits

1 Bit

Picayune

8 Bits

Spanish coins minted in Mexico

Jt was the Age of Exploration. Between the 16th and 19th centuries, the merchants and kings of Europe transported the world's wealth across the seas. England and Spain were the main actors in the drama. The Dutch, Portuguese, French and Italians played supporting roles. Rewards were great but the risks were sometimes greater. Incomplete maps, overloaded ships and primitive navigational instruments made navigation dangerous at best. Very little was known about winds and storm patterns, causing hundreds of premature burial of billions of dollars in gold, silver and precious jewels.

The New England coasts became a virtual graveyard of sunken ships. Three thousand ships sank off the coast of New Hampshire. Seven hundred known shipwreck sites have been identified off Cape Hatteras, North Carolina. From the rocky harbors of Maine to the bayous of Louisiana and throughout the intricate network of Caribbean inlets lie caches of treasure still undiscovered to this day. Even today, following a strong storm along the Atlantic coast, beachcombers will sometimes find a doubloon washed up on the beach, a small reminder of the vast buried storehouses of a golden era. Here are some of the well-known stories of lost treasure which continues to evade even the best modern treasure hunters:

1. The Royal Capitana sank off the coast of Ecuador in the 17th century. Five million dollars worth of treasure lies buried in the sand near Punta Santa Elena.

2. There were the legendary galleons from Manila. For 250 years, large numbers of massive Spanish galleons transported precious cargo from

Lost Treasure

the Philippines to the west coast of Mexico. The overloaded vessels each carried as much as 1-2 thousand tons of gold and silver. It is estimated that several billion dollars in precious metals ended up on the floor of the Pacific Ocean instead of reaching its destination. Much of the lost treasure lies off the coast of Hong Kong.

3. In a naval battle with the English, a fleet of 21 Spanish ships sank just off the coast of Spain in 1656. Even though the site is well documented by ships' logs, Spain to this day will not permit anyone to disturb the ancient burial ground to recover the 1.7 million pieces of eight known to be still resting in the decaying hulls. A separate battle in 1702 sank nearly 40 vessels in Vigo Bay, also near Spain, leaving 3,500 tons of gold and silver still waiting to be recovered.

4. Francis Drake was forced to jettison over 40 tons of gold and silver off the coast of South America to keep his ship from sinking. It has never been found.

5. Captain Kidd buried his fortunes of stolen treasure in the West Indies. No one knows where.

6. Black Bart Roberts buried millions worth of gold on a small island near Sierra Leone. Few have ever tried to locate it.

7. Jean Lafitte left 10 million dollars in loot buried on Galveston Island when he sailed away never to be heard from again.

8. The vast storehouses of Blackbeard's legendary wealth are still missing.

9. And much, much, much, much more . . .

One final note. Before you run to the hardware store for a shovel, remember that much of the world's sunken or buried treasure is strongly protected by governments. It is illegal to dig for some of it, and finding it has its own set of problems. Just ask the pirates.

VEGETABLES

DANDELION GREENS

1 pound raw dandelion greens
1/4 cup butter or oil
1 crushed garlic clove
1 cup chopped onion

1/4 teaspoon cayenne pepper
1/4 teaspoon salt
1/4 teaspoon pepper

Wash and cut greens into one inch strips. Steam until tender (5 minutes). Sauté onions and garlic in butter. Add seasonings. Drain greens and mix into sauteed onions. Simmer five minutes before serving.

CORN PUDDING

4 cups corn (fresh cut from cob, frozen or canned will do). Drain off liquids.
4 eggs (beaten)
1/2 teaspoon salt
1/4 cup diced pimiento
1/4 cup diced bell pepper

1/4 cup diced onion
1 tablespoon diced jalapeño pepper
1/2 cup melted butter
1/2 cup milk
3 cups seasoned bread crumbs or crushed croutons
1/3 cup parmesan cheese

Mix all ingredients but bread crumbs and cheese. Cover bottom of baking dish with 1 1/2 cups of crumbs. Pour corn mix evenly over crumbs. Top with remaining crumbs. Sprinkle with cheese. Bake at 350° for 35 minutes or until cooked through. Serves eight.

VEGETABLES

MAMA'S WILTED LETTUCE

1 pound sliced bacon.
8 cups total of any combination of the following
  uncooked chopped vegetables:
  lettuce
  cabbage
  onions
  celery
  bell peppers
  spinach
  chard
  collard greens
  mushrooms
  1/4 cup water
  1/4 cup soy sauce

Cut bacon into small pieces and fry in large stock pot until almost crisp. Drain off all but 4 tablespoons of fat. Add vegetables and water to bacon. Sauté until wilted. Add soy sauce before serving.

FRENCH GREEN BEANS

4 strips chopped bacon
6-8 cups French green beans (fresh, frozen or
  canned)
1/2 cup minced onion
1/4 teaspoon salt
1/4 teaspoon pepper
1 tablespoon Worcestershire sauce

Fry bacon and discard fat. Sauté onion with bacon till soft. Add beans and seasonings. Cover and simmer for five minutes. Serves six to eight.

VEGETABLES

FRIED EGGPLANT

3 eggplant
1/2 cup oil
3 eggs well beaten
1/2 cup flour
1 cup finely crushed crackers or dried bread
    crumbs

1/4 teaspoon salt
1/4 teaspoon black pepper
1/4 teaspoon oregano
1/4 teaspoon thyme
1/4 teaspoon garlic powder

Peel and slice eggplant into 1/4 inch slices. Soak in salted water for 30 minutes. Dry slices of eggplant. Combine flour, cracker crumbs and spices. Heat oil in fry pan. Dip eggplant in egg, then dip each slice in flour mix. Fry until golden brown on each side. Drain on paper towels. Serve hot.

SQUASH AND PECAN CASSEROLE

4 cups cooked, mashed, acorn squash
1/2 cup chopped pecans
1/4 cup honey or brown sugar
1/4 cup softened butter
2 tablespoons grated orange rind

2 tablespoons orange juice
1 teaspoon cinnamon
1/2 teaspoon salt
1/2 cup whole pecans

Combine all ingredients except whole pecans. Mix well and pour into a two quart casserole. Place whole pecans on top. Bake at 350° for 30 minutes. Serves four to six.

VEGETABLES

SPINACH SOUFFLE

3 cups chopped, steamed spinach (can be fresh or frozen)
1/2 cup butter
3/4 cup flour
2 cups milk

1/2 teaspoon salt
1/4 teaspoon pepper
1 cup grated jack or cheddar cheese
2 beaten eggs

Steam spinach and set aside. Grate cheese and set aside. Melt butter in large sauce pan. Add flour and mix well. Do not brown. Slowly add 2 cups of milk and seasoning. Stir over low heat until thick and smooth. Fold in cheese and eggs. Stir until well blended. Fold in spinach. Pour into greased two quart casserole. Bake 45 minutes at 350° or until golden brown and knife comes out clean when inserted. Serves 6 spinach lovers.

CREOLE TOMATOES AND OKRA

1 pound chopped, sliced bacon
2 crushed garlic cloves
2 cups chopped onion
1 cup chopped celery
1/2 cup chopped green bell peppers
4 cups chopped tomatoes (fresh or canned)
1 teaspoon salt

1/2 teaspoon black pepper
1/2 teaspoon cayenne pepper
3 cups sliced, pre-cooked okra
chicken broth (your choice of canned, fresh or bullion. The amount depends on whether you want to serve this dish like a soup or as a vegetable.)

In a large skillet fry bacon until crispy. Drain off all but two tablespoons of fat. Add garlic, onions and bell pepper. Sauté until tender. Add tomatoes and seasonings. Cover and simmer for 30 minutes. Add okra and broth, then cover and simmer for 30 more minutes. Serves eight.

VEGETABLES

CAULIFLOWER CASSEROLE

1 large cauliflower
2 tablespoons butter
2 tablespoons flour
1 cup milk
1/2 teaspoon salt

1/4 teaspoon white pepper
1/2 cup chopped green onions
1/2 cup chopped mushrooms
1/2 cup cracker crumbs
1/2 cup grated Monterey Jack cheese

Cut cauliflower into bite-size pieces. Steam for about 10 minutes or until tender. Drain. Arrange cauliflower in 8 x 8 baking dish. Melt butter in skillet over medium heat. Stir in flour. Gradually add milk, mixing until smooth. Add seasonings, green onions and mushrooms. Spoon sauce over cauliflower. Mix cracker crumbs and cheese and sprinkle over top. Bake at 375° for 15 minutes. Serves six.

SCALLOPED POTATOES

10-12 medium potatoes
1 tablespoon butter
1 cup chopped onions
1 cup sliced mushrooms

1 tablespoon Worcestershire sauce
1 cup milk
1 cup shredded cheese (your choice)

Prepare roux (see page 10). Peel and thinly slice potatoes. Sauté onions and mushrooms in butter. Add vegetables to roux. Mix thoroughly. Add Worcestershire sauce and milk. Arrange potatoes in a casserole. Pour milk mixture over potatoes. Sprinkle cheese over potatoes. Bake 1 hour at 350°.

The English Serpent

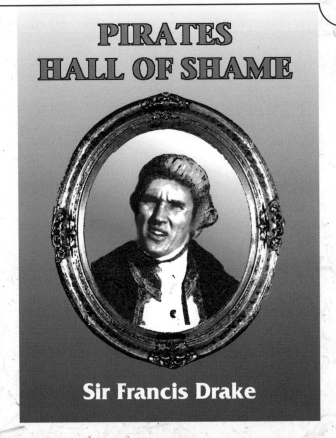

Sir Francis Drake

His life showed great promise. He was vice-admiral when England defeated the Spanish Armada. His name became a national treasure. In his early 20's he earned a reputation as a skilled privateer. In England's eye, Francis Drake could do no wrong and could get any ship and crew he wanted.

Throughout his illustrious career Francis sailed more of the globe than most people knew existed and was the second person to sail completely around the world. His mission was to seek and destroy Spanish vessels and holdings. But somewhere in the fine print of the definition of privateering, Francis got confused. Like a compulsive eater who doesn't seem to know where gluttony begins, Drake pigged out on piracy.

Spain referred to him as "El Dragon," the predator. They saw him as a serpent sinking his fangs into the life blood of Spain. No galleon was safe when the Dragon was on the sea.

One galleon he looted was the *Cacafuego*. It will live forever in the minds of treasure hunters everywhere. So rich was the plunder that it took two gruiling days for both crews to transfer the gold and jewels between the two ships. Once loaded, Drake's smaller ship was so overloaded that the crew had to jettison 50 tons of gold and silver into the ocean just to stay afloat. The treasure has never been found.

The conquests of Francis Drake have forever placed him in the Who's Who of piracy. He pillaged many of the cities of South America and the Caribbean during his illustrious career. When he couldn't capture a city he burned down city blocks forcing a heavy ransom.

His end came when he became gravely ill during a skirmish with the Spanish Armada. He died in bed at the age of 56 and his body was returned to the sea that had made him famous.

6 • FISH
• SEAFOOD

Pirates sailed the oceans and violence ruled the seas. Nations were forced to fortify their once unprotected merchant vessels. As pirate attacks escalated, bigger and more heavily armed warships took to the sea to protect their fleets and hunt down the predators. Disarmament wasn't even a theory in those days.

The cannon was the weapon that turned the tide in many a battle. A typical warship was armed with one hundred of them. They lined the three decks and could send a massive ball of steel crashing into the sails, masts or hulls of their targets. Cannonballs came in all sizes. There was no agency for the standardization of seaboard weapons and no caliber on the guns. It was just cast them in brass or iron as big as possible and then blow your neighbor out of the water. It was the original "Big Bang" theory. Whoever had the biggest and loudest guns could win the prize. Or "Whoever died with the most cannonballs won." The typical sizes of the projectiles fired from the deck guns were 12, 24 and 32 pounds. The 12 pound ball was about the size of a shot put.

The big guns shot 68-pound monsters which could rip out the side of a ship. The large cannonballs were 8 1/2 inches in diameter and traveled through the air the length of 20 soccer fields. Captains' logs record a dozen or more men lost in a single hit from one of these monsters. In the

Weapons and Firepower of Piracy

17th century that was impressive firepower and caused many a smaller fortified ship to surrender or flee in terror. Some guns were mounted on the upper levels and spewed glass, nails and stones on unwelcomed intruders. Other cannons shot red hot balls, heated in a foundry, into enemy sails, setting them on fire. Whether it was the whistle of bird-shot or the deep howl of the 68 pounders, battles at sea were spectacular events and not for the faint-hearted.

Pirates often boarded the ships they were attacking. When they swarmed on board, they were well prepared for hand-to-hand combat. They used axes, swords, daggers, blunderbuss rifles and an array of flintlock handguns. Many pirates carried a saber and as many as six loaded pistols tied to slings which draped over their shoulders. So terrifying was their attack that many victims gave up before the battle even began. It did them little good because pirates had an annoying habit of slaughtering the entire crew. Then they would take the larger and better armed of the two vessels and scuttle the other one. Bigger was always better in the battle for supremacy of the seas.

FRIED SEAFOOD BALLS

Oil for deep frying
1/4 cup butter or oil
1/2 cup chopped onion
1/2 cup chopped celery
1/2 cup chopped mushrooms
1/2 teaspoon salt

1/2 teaspoon cayenne pepper
1 teaspoon minced parsley
2 cups cleaned, chopped or ground seafood
  (your choice)
2 beaten eggs
1 cup bread crumbs

Sauté vegetables in butter or oil. Remove from heat. Add seasonings, seafood, beaten eggs, and bread crumbs. Mix well. If it is not moist enough to hold together, add a small amount of water. Form into balls using 1-2 tablespoons of mixture. Drop into hot oil. Fry for approximately two minutes. Drain on absorbent paper.

SEAFOOD SAUCES

HOT MUSTARD

1 1/2 cups mustard (can use any stone ground,
  but pre-seasoned will not produce true flavor)

1/2 cup mayonnaise
1 tablespoon vinegar
1 tablespoon Tabasco

Mix all ingredients well and refrigerate for at least one hour before serving. Makes two cups.

SMUGGLER'S COVE SAUCE

1 cup mustard, plain or non-seasoned stone
  ground

1/4 cup honey
1/4 cup mayonnaise

Mix all ingredients well and refrigerate for at least one hour before serving. Makes two cups.

ZIPPY COCKTAIL SAUCE

2 cups spicy V-8 juice

1 cup sour cream
1 package onion dip mix

Place all ingredients in a blender, mix until smooth. Refrigerate before serving. Makes three cups.

FISH AND SEAFOOD

MIXED SEAFOOD KABOBS

1 pound lean bacon
2-3 large green bell peppers
2-3 cups cherry tomatoes
2-3 cups pearl onions

2-3 cups whole mushrooms
variety of seafood (shrimp, clams, crab, fish and crawfish) cleaned and cut into bite size pieces

Pre-fry bacon just long enough to remove some of the fat. Drain on absorbent paper until cool. Push skewer through one end of bacon and proceed to alternate vegetables, bacon and seafood, weaving bacon in an S figure between each vegetable and seafood bite. Baste with your choice of sauces from Seafood Section. Place skewers on a baking sheet under broiler until bacon is crisp, turning often to keep from burning. Serve with a variety of sauces.

PORT OF CALL SHRIMP

1 pound sliced and chopped bacon
2 cups uncooked white rice
3 cups hot water
1 cup chopped onions
1 cup chopped celery

1 cup button mushrooms with liquid
1/4 cup Worcestershire sauce
1/2 teaspoon salt
1/4 teaspoon black pepper
2-3 cups cleaned cooked small shrimp

Fry bacon until crispy, drain off all but 2 tablespoons of fat. Return pan to heat. Add rice. Stir constantly to keep bacon and rice from burning. When rice is well-browned, reduce heat and add three cups of hot water, vegetables and seasonings. Cook covered on low heat for 15-20 minutes. Add seafood and cook for an additional five minutes before serving. Serves six.

FISH AND SEAFOOD

CRAB PASTA

1/4 cup butter or oil
6 sliced medium zucchini
1 cup chopped onions
2 minced garlic cloves
1 cup chopped celery
2 cups (1 can) cooked tomatoes
1 can tomato paste

2 bay leaves
1/2 teaspoon salt
1 teaspoon oregano
1/4 teaspoon rosemary
2-3 cups crab meat
1 16 oz. package your choice of pasta noodles

Sauté zucchini, onions, garlic and celery in butter. Add tomato, tomato paste and all seasonings. Cover and simmer on low heat for 30 minutes. Prepare pasta according to directions on package. Add crab meat to vegetables. Simmer 10 minutes more before serving. Serve with French bread and parmesan cheese. Serves six.

FRIED FISH

(This coating mix can be used with any seafood)
Oil for frying
3 pounds of cleaned seafood
2 cups yellow cornmeal
1 cup flour
1 teaspoon salt

1/2 teaspoon cayenne pepper
1/2 teaspoon black pepper
2 cups additional flour
4 beaten eggs
1/2 cup milk

Dry seafood on paper towels. Prepare three separate baking dishes for coating sea foods. Put two cups of flour in the first dish. Mix two cups of cornmeal, one cup of flour, salt and pepper in the second dish. The third dish contains beaten eggs and milk. Place seafood in first baking dish with flour and turn to coat well. Dip seafood in egg and milk mixture, then into 2nd baking dish turning to coat well with cornmeal mix. Place seafood in hot oil and fry until crispy on outside, four to eight minutes depending on size of pieces. Serves six to eight.

FISH AND SEAFOOD

OYSTERS ROCKEFELLER

3 dozen oysters
1 cup chopped green onions
1 cup chopped celery leaves
2 minced garlic cloves
1/2 cup butter
1/2 cup bread crumbs

1 teaspoon salt
one 10-ounce package of frozen chopped
  spinach
1/2 cup parmesan cheese
2 tablespoons Worcestershire

Cook spinach separately and drain off liquid. Sauté onions, celery and garlic in butter. Remove from heat. Stir in bread crumbs, salt, spinach, parmesan cheese and Worcestershire sauce. Remove oysters from shells and clean well. Clean shells and place them on a bed of rock salt in a large baking pan. Place oysters in shells and cover with spinach mixture. Place baking pan in preheated 450° oven for 10-15 minutes or until browned. Serve hot.

CRAWFISH ETTOUFFEE

1/2 cup light roux
1/4 cup butter or oil
1 cup chopped onion
2 minced garlic cloves
1 cup chopped celery
1/2 cup sliced mushrooms

1 cup milk
2 cups water
1/2 teaspoon salt
1/4 teaspoon cayenne pepper
1 pound crawfish meat

Prepare roux (see page 10) and set aside. Sauté vegetables in butter and add roux. Mix well. Slowly blend in milk, water and seasonings. Simmer for 30 minutes. Prepare rice. Add crawfish to pot. Simmer for 10 additional minutes. Serve over rice. Note: for those unfortunate souls who don't have access to crawfish, shrimp may be substituted.

SHRIMP FETTUCCINI

1/2 cup light roux
1/4 cup butter or oil
1 cup chopped onions
1/2 cup chopped bell pepper
2 tablespoons chopped jalapeño pepper
1/2 cup sliced mushrooms
2 cups milk

1/2 teaspoon salt
1/4 teaspoon white pepper
1 cup grated cheese of your choice (cheddar, jack, velveeta)
1 pound cleaned shrimp
1 12-ounce package fettuccini noodles (cooked according to directions)

Prepare roux (see page 10) and set aside. Sauté vegetables in butter. Add roux and slowly stir in milk while simmering. Add seasonings. Fold in cheese and shrimp. Cook on low heat until cheese is melted. Serve over cooked noodles. Serves eight.

STUFFED RED SNAPPER

one 4-6 pound Red Snapper
1/2 cup butter or oil
1 cup chopped onion
1 cup chopped celery
1/4 teaspoon parsley
1/4 teaspoon oregano
1/4 teaspoon thyme
1/2 teaspoon salt
1 teaspoon Tabasco
2 raw eggs

1/4 cup lemon juice
2-3 cups crumbed dried bread (try a variety-corn, French, wheat)
2 cups (1 can) stewed tomatoes with juice
Basting sauce:
1/2 cup butter
1 tablespoon lemon juice
1/4 teaspoon salt
1/4 teaspoon pepper

Clean fish and leave head on. Lay fish in buttered baking dish. Sauté vegetables in butter. Remove from heat and add seasonings, lemon juice, bread crumbs, stewed tomatoes and beaten eggs. If stuffing is not moist enough to hold together, add a small amount of water. Carefully fill fish with stuffing. Baste with sauce before and during baking. Bake at 350° for 45 minutes to one hour.

The Pirate Who Knew When To Quit

Henry Morgan

Crime doesn't pay. Or in the case of pirates it doesn't pay very long. But there was at least one notable exception. His name was Henry Morgan.

Morgan has been referred to by historians as a prince of scoundrels living in an age of scoundrels. He was a British privateer empowered by his nation to destroy England's enemies. It was very obvious he had no one else's blessing.

After one period of successful Spain bashing, Morgan invaded Panama City. Known for its spectacular wooden houses and cathedrals and quaint streets, it was a paradise and one of Central America's most beautiful cities. Morgan assembled a ferocious party of several thousand and invaded the city looking for one thing— precious metals. The residents knew pirates' ways and buried much of their wealth in hidden, underground vaults. Captain Morgan, without mercy, tortured his victims in his attempt to find the treasure. The pirates located only a fraction of the legendary wealth, then burned the city down. But they managed to cart off enough booty to load down 175 mules for the long trek across Panama.

When he arrived back in Jamaica, Morgan was arrested for acts of piracy and sent to England in chains. Arriving home, he was applauded by the Crown and his many friends in parliament. Henry Morgan was knighted and returned to Jamaica as Deputy Governor and, of all things, "Justice of the Peace." The terror of Jamaica had become the Chief of Police. He supposedly saw the error of his former ways and arrested his former pirate crews and associates. Some think he was getting rid of witnesses. The penitent pirate enforced the law with vigor, frequently meting out the death penalty on his partners in crime, referring to them as "vermin." Who would know better?

He died in 1688 at the age of 56, a very wealthy man and honored by his country.

7 · JAMBALAYA
· RICE

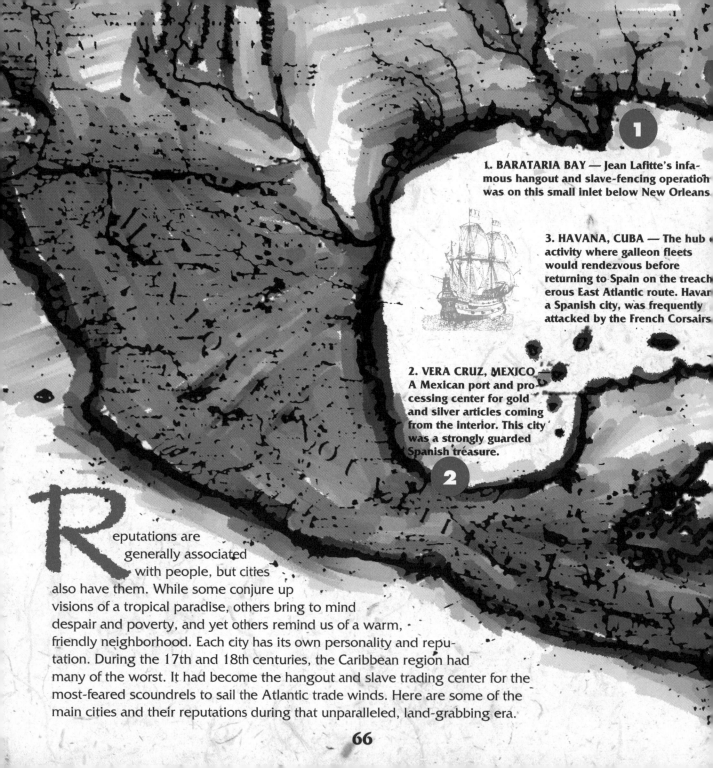

1. BARATARIA BAY — Jean Lafitte's infamous hangout and slave-fencing operation was on this small inlet below New Orleans.

3. HAVANA, CUBA — The hub of activity where galleon fleets would rendezvous before returning to Spain on the treacherous East Atlantic route. Havana, a Spanish city, was frequently attacked by the French Corsairs.

2. VERA CRUZ, MEXICO — A Mexican port and processing center for gold and silver articles coming from the interior. This city was a strongly guarded Spanish treasure.

Reputations are generally associated with people, but cities also have them. While some conjure up visions of a tropical paradise, others bring to mind despair and poverty, and yet others remind us of a warm, friendly neighborhood. Each city has its own personality and reputation. During the 17th and 18th centuries, the Caribbean region had many of the worst. It had become the hangout and slave trading center for the most-feared scoundrels to sail the Atlantic trade winds. Here are some of the main cities and their reputations during that unparalleled, land-grabbing era.

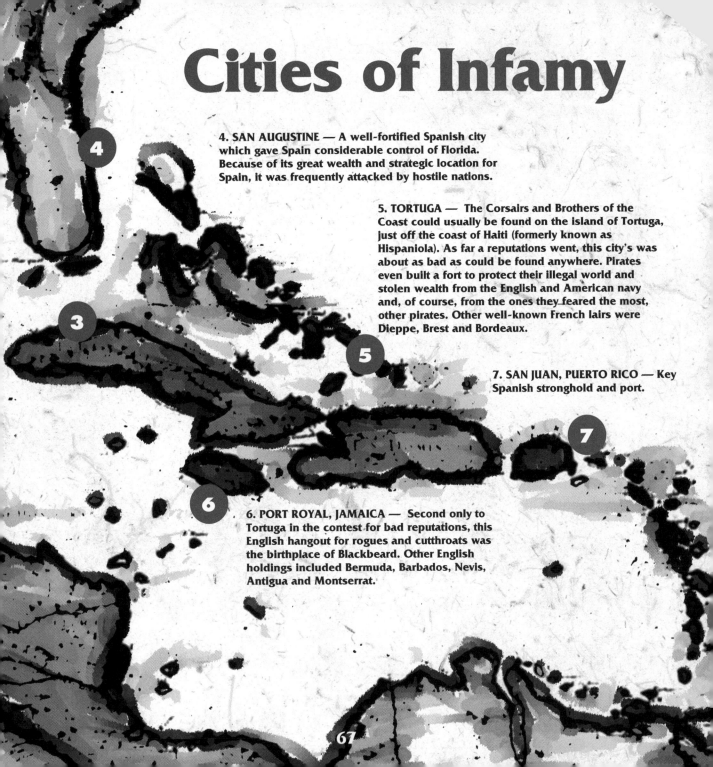

Cities of Infamy

4. SAN AUGUSTINE — A well-fortified Spanish city which gave Spain considerable control of Florida. Because of its great wealth and strategic location for Spain, it was frequently attacked by hostile nations.

5. TORTUGA — The Corsairs and Brothers of the Coast could usually be found on the island of Tortuga, just off the coast of Haiti (formerly known as Hispaniola). As far a reputations went, this city's was about as bad as could be found anywhere. Pirates even built a fort to protect their illegal world and stolen wealth from the English and American navy and, of course, from the ones they feared the most, other pirates. Other well-known French lairs were Dieppe, Brest and Bordeaux.

7. SAN JUAN, PUERTO RICO — Key Spanish stronghold and port.

6. PORT ROYAL, JAMAICA — Second only to Tortuga in the contest for bad reputations, this English hangout for rogues and cutthroats was the birthplace of Blackbeard. Other English holdings included Bermuda, Barbados, Nevis, Antigua and Montserrat.

CHICKEN JAMBALAYA

3 pounds cut up chicken
2 tablespoons butter
1/2 cup chopped bell peppers
1 cup chopped onion
2 crushed garlic cloves
1/2 cup chopped celery

1/2 cup chopped mushrooms
1 cup uncooked white rice
3 cups chicken stock
2 large bay leaves
1 teaspoon salt
1/2 teaspoon white pepper

Cook chicken in five cups of water for one hour, cool and debone chicken. Reserve stock. Sauté peppers, onion, mushroom, garlic and celery in butter. Put chicken, vegetables, rice, stock and seasonings in a large dutch oven or iron skillet. Cover and bake at 350° for 30 minutes or until rice is tender. Serves six.

SEAFOOD JAMBALAYA

1/4 cup dark mahogany roux
1/4 cup butter or oil
1 cup chopped onion
1/2 cup chopped green pepper
2 crushed garlic cloves
1 pound can of tomatoes with juice
2 cups hot water
1 teaspoon thyme

1 teaspoon parsley
1 teaspoon salt
1/4 teaspoon black pepper
1/2 teaspoon red pepper
1 cup uncooked rice
1 cup crabmeat
1 cup chopped oysters
1 cup raw, cleaned shrimp

In a large four quart iron pot prepare roux (see page 10). Sauté onion, bell peppers and garlic in butter. Add tomatoes, water and roux. Stir often while simmering for 10 minutes. Add seasonings, rice and seafood. Cover and cook on low heat for 30 minutes or until rice is tender. Serves 6-8.

CAJUN BEEF AND SAUSAGE JAMBALAYA

3 strips chopped bacon
2 pounds lean beef cut into small chunks
1/2 pound Louisiana smoked, spicy sausage
  (pre-cooked and cut into 1/2 inch slices)
2 crushed garlic cloves
1/2 cup chopped bell pepper

1 cup chopped onion
1/2 cup chopped celery
1 teaspoon salt
1/4 teaspoon black pepper
1 cup uncooked rice
3 cups hot water

Fry bacon in large iron pot, Add beef and sausage. Brown them well in bacon fat. Add garlic, onion, bell pepper, celery, seasonings, rice and water. Cover and cook on low for 30 minutes or until rice is tender. Serves six to eight.

WILD RICE STUFFING

1 pound wild rice
1/2 pound ground or chopped pork sausage
1 cup chopped onion
2 cups sliced mushrooms

1 tablespoon minced parsley
1 teaspoon thyme
1 teaspoon salt
1/2 teaspoon white pepper

Cook wild rice according to directions on package until almost tender. Brown pork sausage. Drain off fat. Saute onion, mushrooms and seasonings with sausage. Combine with rice. Mix well. Loosely stuff poultry or meat with mixture. Roast meat according to directions for meat.

JAMBALAYA AND RICE

PAW PAW'S DIRTY RICE

1 pound chicken or turkey gizzards
1/2 pound chicken or turkey livers
1/2 pound ground pork
1 cup chopped onion
1 cup chopped green pepper
1 cup chopped celery
1 teaspoon salt

1/2 teaspoon cayenne pepper
1/2 teaspoon black pepper
3 minced garlic cloves
1 cup chopped green onions
4 cups cooked white rice
1 cup water or any stock

Grind or chop fine the gizzards and liver. Brown all meats in large iron pot. Add onion, garlic, green pepper, celery, seasonings and water. Simmer this mixture for 15 minutes. Add four cups of cooked rice and green onions to meat mixture. Continue to cook on low heat until all liquid is absorbed. Serves eight to ten.

RED BEANS AND RICE

1 pound dry red beans
1 teaspoon salt
1 cup chopped onion
1/2 cup chopped bell pepper
2 crushed garlic cloves
1/2 cup chopped celery

2 bay leaves
1 teaspoon cayenne pepper
1 teaspoon black pepper
1 pound smoked ham chunks or 1 pound spicy
  sausage cut in 1/2 inch thick slices

Clean and soak beans overnight. In morning rinse beans and cover with salted water. Cover and cook for 2 hours. Add onion, bell pepper, garlic, celery, bay leaves, spices and meat. Cover and simmer on low for two hours or until beans are soft. Prepare white rice. Serves eight.

No More Mr. Nice Guy!

Some say that when L'olonnois was born, the doctor slapped his mother. Someone has to be the worst—in this scoundrel's case there was little competition.

Born an indentured servant in the West Indies, he grew up with a grudge against the human race. After spending his early years as a drifter, he linked up with the brutal French Corsairs and he was finally home.

It didn't take long to build a reputation as a heartless murderer, making his mark in piracy by inhuman tortures often slaughtering entire crews. He amassed large stolen fortunes and squandered them just as quickly with his notorious gambling. So it was back to the pirate seas to help support his drinking and gambling habits.

L'olonnois' wasn't a biased man; he hated everyone! To enforce obedience of a group of Spanish prisoners, he once tied up one of his unfortunate captives and in the presence of all the men, cut the man's heart out and ate it while it was still beating as a warning that anyone who resisted him would meet the same fate. The man who began as a slave became a dark lord among the French buccaneers, commanding hundreds of bloodthirsty pirates. He became known as the most vicious of all who ever tormented the Caribbean.

His end came dramatically when he lost a battle to a strong Spanish regiment on the island of Las Perlas, near Venezuela. Surviving the attack, he

PIRATES HALL OF SHAME

L'olonnois

fled with the remaining crew into the waiting arms of the island's Carib Indians. The Caribs were cannibals and turned history's most vicious pirate into gumbo for the evening supper. They probably had heartburn for weeks.

8 · CREOLES
· BISQUES

Pirate Logos

Businesses and corporations frequently use symbols to establish their presence. The trademark or logo can be an important part of the corporate identity and represents the personality and integrity of a company. Countries and shipping enterprises during the 17th and 18th centuries identified their cause by coats of arms, carved figures, painted designs and flags.

It might have been expected that the buccaneers would develop their distinguishing mark as well. After all, no one likes an identity crisis, not even pirates.

The flag of the pirate was called a "Roger" or a "Jolly Roger." It was normally characterized by a skull and crossed bones. Some used images of weapons instead. Their black and white emblem, like a corporate logo, came to characterize the personality and integrity of the bearer. Whereas most trademarks are designed to communicate security and stability, this one meant chaos and death. The only use society has found for the skull and crossed bones is to label bottles of poison.

Each pirate had his own personalized version of the Jolly Roger. Each wanted to be unique and not use another's business card. As proud as they were of their flags, sometimes a pirate would hide the Jolly Roger and fly an English or Spanish flag in order to gain access to a harbor without resistance.

Once given safe passage, they would raise their symbol of terror again as they attacked.

Pictured are a few samples of the Jolly Rogers which many a West Indies crew wished they had never seen.

JOLLY ROGER LEGEND

1. Blackbeard
2. Emanuel Wynne
3. Walter Kennedy
4. Henry Every
5. Edward Low
6. Edward England
7. Christopher Moody
8. Stede Bonnet
9. Thomas Tew
10. Richard Worley
11. Bartholomew Roberts
12. "Calico Jack" Rackam

CRAB VEGETABLE BISQUE

1/2 cup white roux
1/4 cup butter
1 cup chopped green onions
1/2 cup chopped celery (use leafy part)
1 pint light cream or evaporated milk
1 quart chicken stock
2 bay leaves

1/2 teaspoon salt
1/4 teaspoon white pepper
1/2 cup fresh or frozen green peas
1/2 cup fresh or frozen broccoli
1/2 cup fresh or frozen corn
2 cups white crab meat

Prepare roux (see page 10). Sauté onions and celery in butter. Add roux, cream or milk, chicken stock and seasonings. Simmer for 20 minutes. Add vegetables. Simmer for 20 minutes. Add crab meat and simmer for 10 more minutes. Serve with French bread. Serves eight.

CLASSIC SHRIMP CREOLE

1/4 cup medium roux
1 pound medium shrimp, peeled and deveined
1/4 cup oil or butter
1 cup chopped onion
2 minced garlic cloves
1/2 cup chopped green peppers
2 cups peeled cooked tomatoes

1/2 cup chopped celery
1/2 cup sliced mushrooms
1 teaspoon salt
1/2 teaspoon black pepper
1 teaspoon Tabasco sauce
2 bay leaves

Bring two quarts of salted water to a boil and cook shrimp for five minutes. Reserve water. When shrimp is cool, peel and devein. Prepare roux (see page 10). Sauté onion, garlic, green peppers, tomatoes, celery and mushroom in oil or butter. Add seasonings and 1/2 of the shrimp stock. Add roux. Add more stock to produce a thin soup. Simmer for one hour. Prepare rice. Add shrimp to soup 5 minutes before serving. Remove bay leaves and serve over rice. Serves six to eight.

CREOLES AND BISQUES

CHICKEN CREOLE

one 3-pound chicken cut into serving pieces
2 bay leaves
1/2 cup medium roux
1/4 cup butter or oil
1 cup chopped onion
1 cup chopped celery

2 minced garlic cloves
1/2 cup sliced mushrooms
4 cups canned tomatoes
1/2 teaspoon salt
1/4 teaspoon thyme
1/2 teaspoon black pepper

Cook chicken in four cups of water with bay leaves for 1/2 hour. Prepare roux (see page 10). Sauté onion, garlic, celery and mushrooms in 1/4 cup of butter or oil. Blend in roux and tomatoes. Add chicken, seasoning and stock. Simmer for 1/2 hour. Serve with white rice. Serves eight.

HAM BISQUE

1/2 cup dark mahogany roux
1/4 cup oil or butter
1 cup chopped onion
2 minced garlic cloves
1 cup chopped turnips
2 cups chopped carrots

2 cups chicken broth
2 cups canned tomatoes
1/2 teaspoon salt
1/4 teaspoon black pepper
1/4 teaspoon oregano
2 cups chopped smoked ham

Prepare roux (see page 10). Sauté onion, garlic, turnips, carrots in 1/4 cup of oil or butter. Add broth and roux. Simmer for 20 minutes. Add tomatoes, spices and ham. Simmer another 20 minutes. Serves six.

CRAWFISH BISQUE

1/2 cup dark mahogany roux
2 pounds crawfish
1/4 cup butter or oil
1 1/2 cup minced onion
1 cup minced celery
2 minced garlic cloves
1/2 cup minced green onions
1/2 cup minced green pepper
1/4 cup minced parsley

2 cups mashed canned tomatoes
1 cup bread crumbs
2 beaten eggs
1 teaspoon thyme
1 teaspoon salt
1/2 teaspoon pepper
1/2 teaspoon cayenne pepper
2 bay leaves

Prepare roux (see page 10) and set aside. Cook crawfish in three quarts of salted boiling water for 20 minutes. Remove crawfish and set water aside. When crawfish have cooled, remove meat. Clean heads well and set aside for stuffing. Sauté onion, celery, garlic, green onions, green pepper, parsley and tomatoes in 1/4 cup of butter or oil. Mince meat of crawfish and add to vegetable mix. Add bread crumbs, eggs and all spices except bay leaves. Stuff three dozen clean heads with mixture. Place on baking sheet and bake at 350° for 10 minutes. Blend roux into remaining vegetable/meat mix. Add enough of water from crawfish to make a thick soup. Simmer for one hour. Prepare white rice. 10 minutes before serving add stuffed heads. Serve over rice. Serves six to eight.

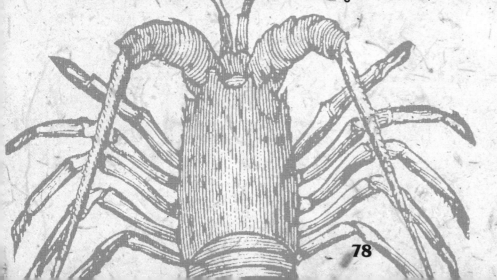

The Pirate who Wanted to be King

Jonathan Lambert

Most pirates were satisfied with the basics like fame, fortune and adventure. Jonathan Lambert was not like most pirates. He wanted more. He wanted power. He wanted to be the king of his own personal empire. And that is what he was, at least for a short while.

Jonathan was a successful pirate and had no problem seizing five islands in the South Atlantic. Shortly after, he placed an official proclamation of sovereignty in a New England newspaper. King Lambert then proceeded to live out his dream on the newly founded "Isles of Refreshment," a nation whose chief occupations were drinking and carousing. A formula for success it was not. But Jonathan was King, and the empire did exist.

Government funding for this new sovereign nation was provided by piracy. Looted vessels helped fill government coffers and make its king rich. Lambert's plan was to provide a mid-ocean, tropical paradise pit stop for weary merchant crews and a place where needed supplies could be purchased by all traders of the Atlantic route. Unfortunately, Lambert was a better buccaneer than businessman, and his entrepreneurial ideas fizzled out one by one. Each business venture resulted in deficit spending, requiring new taxation on all passing ships. Underpaid crews mutinied and abandoned the paradise project. The King lost credibility and subjects.

In desperation King Lambert went on one final expedition, leaving one drunk sailor to guard his island oasis. His ship never returned. Only speculation remains about that fateful voyage. When the British finally arrived to secure the kingdom, the lonely, deserted sailor told of great riches buried on the island but then mysteriously died before he could reveal the location. A volcanic eruption later permanently buried the treasure and the last remains of King Lambert's paradise.

9

- **BREADS**
- **BISCUITS**
- **FRITTERS**

This painting was inspired by classic, 19th Century artist, Howard Pyle.

Because they operated outside the law of the land, it is often falsely assumed that the pirates had no law at all. It is true that they were a law unto themselves, but there was a law. Codes of acceptable pirate behavior for the most part governed the rebel bands. They also had fairly detailed procedures for dealing with violators.

Executions were carried out quickly by saber or rope. The most infamous device of pirate justice has become more of a product of journalistic exaggeration than an actual practice of the times. The feared "plank" was only rarely used, but its terrifying legend remains. Much more common than the plank in the pirate judicial system was the practice of marooning the accused on a desolate island with only a small amount of provision to prolong the agony.

The Custom of the Coast

One well-known pirate code was called

Scalliwag Codes and "the Plank"

the Custom of the Coast. All members of the Brothers of the Coast had to vow to strictly follow the code in order to belong to the Brotherhood (or better, the brother hoods). The code was the law for the lawless which helped the French Brothers keep some semblance of order in their free-for-all lifestyle.

The code established a system for a democratic election of ship's officers and defined how the spoils of piracy were to be divided. There was also a fairly detailed description of how to punish those who violated the code. Here are some highlights from the Custom of the Coast:

No brother could steal from another or he would have his ears and nose cut off. If he had a second offense, he was marooned on a deserted island.

A man who would be elected captain had to display obvious leadership strengths, and be experienced and fearless in battle.

Every member of the crew was given a portion of the loot according to his importance in rank. Captains got five shares, officers two shares and each member of the crew received one share.

Young people today enjoy playing the game "Capture the Flag." The game's roots date back to pirate days. The Custom of the Coast provided for special rewards for any crew member who captured the enemy's flag.

Special compensations were given for injuries incurred in battle. The loss of a hand was compensated with 600 pieces of eight or six slaves. An eye was worth 100 pieces of eight or one slave.

When a Brother was marooned on a deserted island, he was shown a degree of mercy. He was given a bottle of water and a musket with ammunition.

Special commendation was afforded those who showed high marksmanship abilities, and a reward was always given to the one who first spotted an enemy ship.

There was even a provision for kidnapped prisoners. They were given a small part of the spoils of battle. History does reveal, however, that not all prisoners were treated according to the code. Somehow that doesn't surprise us.

BREADS AND FRITTERS

BANANA FRITTERS

1 cup flour
1 teaspoon baking powder
1/4 teaspoon salt
1 teaspoon cinnamon
1 beaten egg

1/3 cup milk
3 ripe mashed bananas
Enough hot oil for deep frying
Confectioners sugar

Sift flour, baking powder, salt and cinnamon together. Blend together egg, milk and mashed banana. Fold into flour mixture. Drop by spoonfuls into hot oil (350°). Cook until golden brown. Drain on absorbent paper. Dust with confectioners sugar. Makes two dozen.

RICE FRITTERS

1/4 cup sugar
1 tablespoon butter
3 eggs
1 cup cold cooked rice
1 cup flour
1/2 teaspoon salt

1 tablespoon baking powder
1/2 teaspoon nutmeg
1/2 teaspoon cinnamon
Enough oil for deep frying
1 cup confectioners sugar

Cream sugar, butter and eggs. Blend in rice until light and fluffy. Sift together all remaining ingredients. Fold into creamed rice mixture. In a deep skillet heat oil to 350°. Drop batter by tablespoons into hot oil. Fry until golden brown. Drain on absorbent paper. Dust with confectioners sugar. Makes two dozen. Serve with Cafe au Lait.

BREADS AND FRITTERS

NEW ORLEANS FRENCH TOAST

1 loaf French bread. Prepare in 1/2 inch thick
  slices. Leave out to dry for one day.
4 well-beaten eggs
1 cup milk
1/2 teaspoon vanilla extract

1/4 teaspoon cinnamon
1/4 teaspoon nutmeg
butter
confectioners sugar
syrup

Blend eggs, milk, vanilla, cinnamon and nutmeg together. Heat griddle to 350°. Melt two tablespoons of butter on griddle. Dip bread into egg mixture, then fry on griddle, turning to brown both sides. Dust with confectioners sugar. Serve with butter and syrup. Serves four to six.

CRACKLIN' BONES CORN BREAD

1 cup corn meal
3/4 cup flour
1/2 teaspoon salt
1 teaspoon baking soda
2 cups buttermilk

1 well-beaten egg
1 cup crumbled cracklins or crispy fried bacon
(For a spicy version add 1/4 cup minced jalapeño
  peppers.)

Mix all dry ingredients except cracklins and peppers. Add milk and eggs. Mix only until blended. Fold in cracklins (and peppers if desired). Pour into well-greased iron skillet, baking pan or muffin tins. Bake 20 minutes at 450°.

BREADS AND FRITTERS

DUMPLINGS

1 1/2 cups flour
4 teaspoons baking powder
1/2 teaspoon salt

1 beaten egg
2/3 cup milk

Mix all dry ingredients. Combine egg and milk. Add to dry ingredients. Mix well. Drop by spoonfuls into 6 cups of boiling broth or gravy. Cover and reduce heat. Simmer for 20 minutes. Serves six.

SOUTHERN BISCUITS

2 cups all purpose flour
1/2 teaspoon salt
3 teaspoons baking powder

6-7 tablespoons cold butter, lard or shortening
(or combination of the three)
3/4 cup milk

Combine dry ingredients. Add butter, lard or shortening. Mix well with fingers or a pastry cutter until consistency of coarse meal. Mix in milk until dough forms a ball. On a floured surface knead dough about 10 times. Pat dough to 1/2 inch thick. Cut into desired shapes with knife or sharp biscuit cutter. Place biscuits on ungreased cookie sheets. Bake in preheated 375° oven for 10 minutes or until lightly browned. Makes one dozen.

BREADS AND FRITTERS

SPOON BREAD

1 cup water
2 cups milk
1 cup cornmeal
1/2 teaspoon salt

2 tablespoons butter
1 tablespoon baking powder
3 eggs separated

Beat egg whites until stiff, set aside. Stir cornmeal into one cup of water and one cup of milk. Cook slowly until it is thick and smooth. Remove from heat and beat in salt, baking powder, butter, remaining milk and well-beaten egg yolks. Fold in the stiff egg whites. Turn into greased 2 quart baking dish. Bake 30 minutes at 350°.

HUSHPUPPIES

1 1/2 cups corn meal
1/2 cup flour
2 teaspoons baking powder
1 teaspoon salt
1 egg
3/4 cup milk

Variations
To make sweet add 2 teaspoons of sugar
To make spicy add 1/2 cup chopped onion and
     1/4 cup of finely chopped jalapeño pepper

Combine all dry ingredients. Beat egg in milk and add at once. Mix well. Let it set for 5 minutes. Drop by spoonfuls into hot fat (375°). Fry until light golden brown. Drain on paper towels. Serve with fish and tartar sauce. Makes two dozen.

TRADITIONAL FRENCH BREAD

2 packages yeast
1/2 cup luke warm water
1 tablespoon salt
1 teaspoon sugar

2 cups lukewarm water
7 cups flour
1 beaten egg
1 tablespoon water

Dissolve two packages of yeast in 1/2 cup of lukewarm water. Let it stand for five minutes. Add sugar and salt. Stir in two cups of lukewarm water and flour. Mix until it forms a ball. Turn onto a well-floured board and knead for 10 minutes until smooth and elastic. Add small amounts of flour when needed. Put into a greased bowl, cover and let it rise for about 1 1/2 hours or until it doubles in size. Punch dough down and let it rise a second time. Turn onto a floured board. Divide in half and shape into two long loaves. Place on a cookie sheet that has been greased and sprinkled with cornmeal. Slit diagonally every two inches. Let them rise until doubled in size. Brush with mixture of one beaten egg and one tablespoon of water. Bake in the oven for 40 minutes at 375°. Brush loaves again with egg mixture. Continue baking for 10-15 minutes more. Cool before serving.

Not Just a Man's World

Mary Read

Even in the liberated 20th century there are still some roles in which women are not quickly accepted. Piracy is one such role. As early as the 16th century, however, Lady Kiligrew of England led a pirate crew which plundered a German vessel, killed the entire crew and escaped with the spoils. Her tradition was later carried on by Mary Read.

Mary began her life as a boy. Mary's mother made her play the role of a son so she could get an inheritance. It was a part Mary played so well she did it the rest of her life. It was a man's world. Mary wanted all of it she could get. Her masquerade eventually led her into the Royal British Military and she became skilled in fighting and weaponry. None ever suspected "she" was not a "he."

A romantic interest led to a disaster, and she joined a Dutch privateering vessel to get away from the world she knew. She soon developed the reputation of a feared fighter. But romance again caused problems for her. She fell in love with one of the sailors and revealed to him that she was not a man. As her involvement grew, her lover was challenged to a duel by one of the crew. Knowing that her lover would die at the ruffian's hand, Mary made a desperate attempt to save his life. Without her lover's knowledge Mary picked a fight with the brute and challenged him to a duel. It worked. Mary shot him and finished him with her sword.

Later, Mary married her man and the masquerade was over. Before they could return to England and settle down, she was captured and tried for piracy. Testimony of the crew described her as the most bloodthirsty on the ship. She even shot her own fellow crew members who displayed cowardice in battle. She was sentenced to hang, but because she was pregnant, was imprisoned instead. There she died of a fever along with her unborn baby. History would soon teach that Mary Read was not the last of the women pirates.

10
POULTRY

Man has usually found a way to justify his actions no matter how vile they are. Even the capture and sale of African slaves became an accepted practice by many for hundreds of years. The Dutch were the first to enter the human merchandise market. They were quickly followed by England, Germany and Sweden. It didn't take long before the pirates caught on that there was big money to be made supplying greedy plantation owners with large numbers of cheap slave labor. The entire West Indies economy and that of the southern United States became dependent on the stolen workers from Africa. The market value on the Caribbean plantations was one dollar per pound for this human contraband.

Few seemed to be bothered by the hardships placed on African families when children were stripped from their mothers' arms and young men and women were dragged like chained dogs into the cramped holds of cargo ships to be forever separated from loved ones and family. Many of them died in their dark, overcrowded prison holds during the treacherous Atlantic crossing. They weren't transported like workers; they were handled like animals. If they survived and reached the New World, many spent the rest of their lives in fear of paddles, chains, whips and thumbscrews. They were abused victims in a greed war that placed property above humanity.

The total number of slaves in the Caribbean is difficult to estimate, but there were millions of them. The slave population in the southern United States grew from 700,000 in 1790 to 4,000,000 by 1860. It was called supply and demand and the pirates wanted to control the supply industry. The most famous of the slave smugglers were the Lafitte boys in New Orleans. They set up their own camps to process and distribute large numbers of slaves to southern plantation owners. Even though the practice was illegal, the Lafittes were immune to any real prosecution because the entire economy of the South was dependent on the slave trade.

Even though slavery was outlawed in the United States in 1808, it took another 50 years for the practice to be eradicated. Of all the atrocities the pirates participated in, none has left deeper scars than their role in the slave trade.

The 17th and 18th century, slave trade was part of a massive trade triangle. Slaves were captured and transported to the West Indies to work on sugar cane plantations. Molasses was shipped to New England and then rum was sent to Africa.

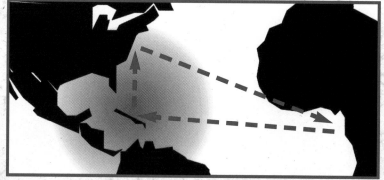

Black Ivory

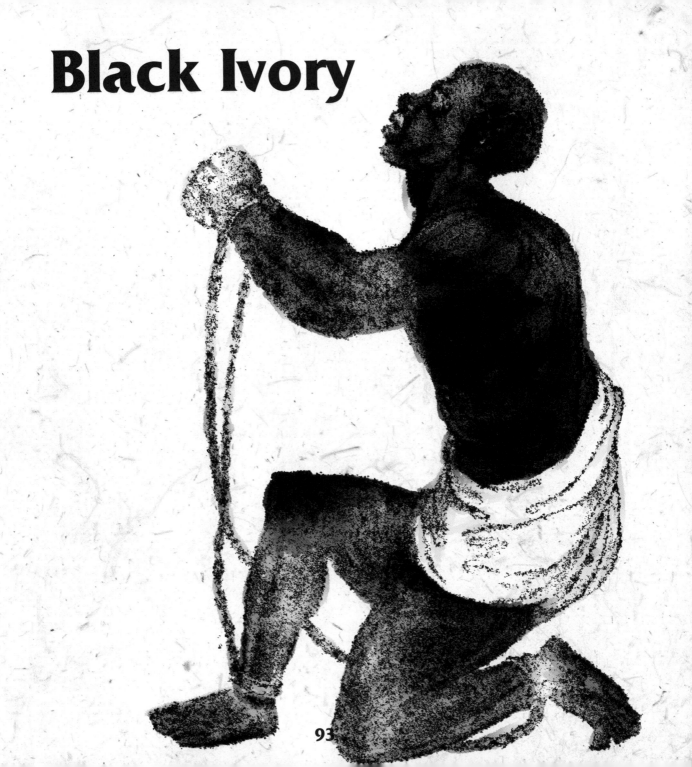

POULTRY

CUTTHROAT DAN'S CHICKEN

one 3-pound chicken per 5 people
1 cup tomato sauce
1/2 cup light molasses
2 minced garlic cloves

1 tablespoon Tabasco
1 teaspoon salt
1 tablespoon Worcestershire sauce
1 teaspoon ginger

Cut chicken into 10 serving size pieces. Combine all other ingredients. Marinate chicken overnight in sauce, or at least four hours. Drain off excess sauce before cooking chicken under broiler or on BBQ. Baste with sauce during cooking. Cook approximately 40 minutes. Turn to keep from burning.

GULF OF MEXICO FRIED CHICKEN

one 3-pound chicken for every 5 people
2 cups flour per chicken
1 teaspoon salt
1/2 teaspoon garlic powder

1/2 teaspoon black pepper
1/4 teaspoon cayenne pepper
2 cups oil for frying

Clean and cut up chicken into 8 or 10 pieces. Giblets can also be prepared and fried. They add flavor while frying. Pour flour and seasonings into a large paper or plastic bag. Close and shake to mix. Drop chicken pieces one at a time into flour and gently shake to coat. Remove chicken onto a clean, dry surface. When all chicken is coated repeat coating process if there is any flour mix left. Leave coated chicken on a clean dry surface while preheating oil to 350° in a large heavy skillet. Carefully place chicken in oil. It should bubble rapidly if it is hot enough. Turn chicken as each side browns. Chicken should be tender inside in approximately 30 minutes. Drain on absorbent paper. Serve hot or cold.

ORANGE GARLIC CHICKEN

2 pounds skinless/boneless chicken breast

Sauce:
- 3 minced garlic cloves
- 1/2 cup orange juice
- 1/2 teaspoon salt
- 1/4 teaspoon white pepper
- 1/8 teaspoon ground ginger

2 tablespoons butter
1 1/2 cups cold water
2 tablespoons corn starch
1 teaspoon sugar

Cut chicken into bite-size pieces. Combine orange juice, garlic, salt and pepper to make sauce. Marinate overnight or at least for four hours in sauce. Drain excess sauce and set aside. Sauté chicken in two tablespoons of butter for 10 minutes. To excess sauce add cold water, two tablespoons of corn starch and one teaspoon of sugar. Add to chicken and cook on medium heat until it thickens. Serve over white rice. Serves six to eight.

TANGY CHICKEN MARINADE

2 pounds skinless boneless chicken breast

Sauce:
- 1/2 cup lime juice
- 1 tablespoon Tabasco
- 1 teaspoon salt

Marinate chicken overnight or at least for four hours in sauce. Drain excess sauce from chicken and use to baste chicken while cooking. Chicken can be B-B-Q'd or broiled.

POULTRY

BAKED CHICKEN

one 3-pound chicken per 5 people
1 teaspoon salt
1/2 teaspoon white pepper

1/2 teaspoon garlic powder
1/2 cup melted butter
1/4 cup lemon juice

Preheat oven to 350°. Carefully clean chicken leaving it whole if you want to stuff it. You can also cut it into serving pieces before baking. *If baking a cut-up chicken*, place pieces in glass baking dish. Combine all other ingredients and baste chicken well before placing in oven. Baste every 15 minutes for one hour or until chicken is tender. *To stuff whole chicken*, Prepare Wild Rice Stuffing. When chicken has been cleaned and stuffing has cooled sufficiently to handle, loosely stuff cavity of chicken. Place chicken breast-side-up in glass baking dish or roasting pan. Baste with sauce mix and place in oven. Baste every 15 minutes. Bake stuffed chicken 30 minutes for every pound. When done, leg should move loosely at joint.

KING EDWARD'S ROAST DUCK

1 duck approximately 6 pounds or two 3-pound
 ducks
1 teaspoon salt

1/4 teaspoon black pepper
Wild Rice Stuffing

Clean and dress duck. Rub inside and out with seasonings. Stuff cavities of duck with Wild Rice Stuffing and stitch or pin closed. Place duck, breast-side-up in a roasting pan or baking dish. Cover and bake at 350° for three hours if using one 6-pound duck and two hours if using two 3-pound ducks.

POULTRY

ROAST DUCK WITH APPLE

2 ducks
1 teaspoon salt
4-5 Pippin or Granny Smith apples
1/2 cup medium roux

2 cups pure apple juice
1/2 teaspoon ground cloves
1/2 teaspoon ground cinnamon
6 peeled, sliced, sweet potatoes

Clean ducks and rub with salt. Cut into serving pieces or split in half and place in a greased baking dish, meaty side up. Roast in 400° oven for 20 minutes. Core apples and slice in rings. Prepare roux (see page 10). Slowly add heated apple juice and seasonings to roux. Remove baking dish from oven and pour off any fat. Pour roux mix over duck. Arrange apple slices and sweet potatoes over and around duck. Cover and bake for one hour at 350°. Serves six.

MUSHROOM CHICKEN

one 3-pound chicken
1/2 teaspoon salt
4 cups water
1/2 cup dark mahogany roux
1/4 cup butter or oil

1 large onion sliced in rings
1 cup fresh sliced mushrooms
3 tablespoons Worcestershire sauce
1/2 teaspoon black pepper

Clean and cut chicken into serving pieces. Cover and cook in four cups of water for 30 minutes. Chicken will not be tender yet. Prepare roux (see page 10). Set aside. Sauté onions and mushrooms in butter. Add to roux. Add hot chicken broth. Stir gently until well blended. Add chicken and seasonings. Simmer for 30 minutes more. Serve with white rice.

POULTRY

PIERRE LE GRANDE LIME CHICKEN

3 pounds of chicken breasts, thighs and drum-
sticks (skins removed)
2 minced garlic cloves
1/2 cup lime juice
1 teaspoon salt
1/8 teaspoon white pepper
1/4 cup oil

1/2 cup flour
2 bay leaves
1/4 cup brown sugar
1 onion, quartered
4 potatoes, peeled and quartered
1 cup water

Combine garlic, lime, salt, pepper and sugar. Marinate chicken for four hours in this mixture, turning often. Heat oil in large deep skillet. Remove chicken from marinade and set sauce aside. Dust chicken on all sides with flour. Brown chicken in hot oil. Add onion, bay leaves, potatoes, water and marinade. Cover and simmer for 45 minutes or until chicken is tender. Serve with white rice. Serves six.

CORNISH HENS WITH MANGO SAUCE

6 Cornish hens
salt and pepper
3-4 ripe mangos

1/2 teaspoon ginger
1/2 teaspoon cinnamon
2 tablespoons melted butter

Heat oven to 325°. Rub Cornish hens with salt and pepper. Arrange in baking dish. Scoop flesh from mangoes. Blend on medium speed with ginger, cinnamon and butter. Pour sauce over hens. Bake, uncovered for 45 minutes or until tender. Baste often. Serve with white rice. Serves six.

Terror on the New England Coast

Blackbeard

Lured by the mystique and adventure of high seas privateering, Edward Teach seemed like just another teenage runaway. History would prove him to be different.

Edward had a voice like a cannon and his 6'4" 250-pound frame soon cleared a path of fear on the pirate seas. His full, black beard extending to his waist became his calling card. The name "Blackbeard" became the best-known title in pirate history, and *The Queen Anne's Revenge*, the most feared vessel from Venezuela to Maine.

To his victims he was treacherous; to his crew he was mean; and the 14 most unfortunate women of that time were his wives, many of whom starved to death locked up in his treasure room. He would hold cities at siege while he robbed incoming ships, exacting illegal tolls and taxes on the merchant vessels. During his reign of terror much of the trade was stopped in the northern colonies.

Blackbeard's Jolly Roger which identified his pirate vessel.

One of Blackbeard's practices was to tie burning matches in his beard so it was smoldering when he boarded his terrified victims' vessels. He was an intimidating figure to all who encountered him, all except one man, Lieutenant Robert Maynard of His Majesty's Navy. Maynard tracked the elusive villain to Ocracoke Inlet in North Carolina, where he engaged him in a bloody hand-to-hand battle in the chilly, November air of 1718. With five bullets in Blackbeard's body, and bleeding from 20 severe cutlass slashes, the murderer who claimed he would outlive the Devil, breathed his last.

In the tradition of David and Goliath, Lieutenant Maynard cut the head off the giant and proudly displayed his trophy when he sailed home. The new hero collected his reward, and the remaining cutthroats of Blackbeard's crew were hanged.

11

- PORK
- SAUSAGE

Life at Sea

Something about the sea—gentle breezes, distant lands and the adventure of a lifetime—beckons the soul. Unfortunately, dreams of romance and riches often turned to nightmares in the 17th and 18th centuries. When the sails were finally unfurled, the wind and merciless sea became the master. Journeys which should have taken weeks often turned into months, and some became eternities.

In that era, crossing the Pacific Ocean from West to East took as long as six months. A voyage around the world took 18 months and the journey was treacherous at best. The bilges in the leaking vessels were constantly filled with water. The stench from the holds was overwhelming because they frequently served as toilets. Men worked around the clock and slept when they could on the hardwood decks and holds. Rats roamed freely and contaminated the food rations. Tempers often flared in the stinking, overcrowded conditions made even more unbearable by frequent food shortages. Fleas and lice were everyone's bed mates.

Food spoilage was frequently the biggest hindrance to a successful voyage. Biscuits and grain commonly fell victim to weevils and roaches. Once sour, it became inedible. The following entry in Magellan's journal describes the situation faced by many a sailor attempting to cross the great oceans:

> "We ate only biscuit reduced to powder, and full of grubs, and stinking from the dirt which the rats had made on it when eating the good biscuit, and we drank water that was yellow and stinking. We also ate the ox hides which were under the main-yard, also the sawdust of wood, and rats."

Food shortages frequently caused captains to leave their planned route to search small islands for new food supplies. These island detours sometimes ended in disaster when the local native population viewed the arriving crew as their meal for the night. If pirates and natives didn't do them, the constant onslaught of diseases often did. Malnutrition and scurvy weakened the crew, often leading to other diseases. A shortage of clean drinking water inevitably brought on typhoid and cholera, and inoculations were unknown back then. A voyage was considered successful if only one in five died from disease. It wasn't uncommon to find a fellow sailor who had died during the night half eaten by rats.

Shipboard duties were dangerous, and serious injuries were a part of the job description of the 17th century sailor. Untreated wounds became gangrenous. Broken bones were treated without the advantages of proper equipment or good medical procedures. And if that wasn't enough, there was the ever-present threat that they would be raided by an equally desperate and starving band of pirates looking for loot and food. Shakespeare referred to them as "whoreson, beetle-headed, flapear'd knaves." By the time a journey ended the idea of gentle breezes, distant lands and the adventure of a lifetime had been replaced with reality. If the sailors were fortunate to reach the New World you can be certain none of them went to work for a travel agency.

TRADE WINDS PORK CHOPS

2 pounds thick pork chops
1 sliced large onion
2 tart apples cut in thin wedges
1/4 cup molasses

1 cup water
1/2 teaspoon salt
1/4 teaspoon black pepper

Brown chops well on both sides in heavy skillet. Cover with onions and apples. Mix together water, molasses, salt and pepper. Pour over chops. Cover and simmer 30-45 minutes or until tender. Serve with rice.

PORK STEAMED CABBAGE

1 head cabbage
1 tablespoon butter
2 cups sliced sausage or chopped smoked ham

1/2 teaspoon salt
1/4 teaspoon black pepper
1/2 cup hot water

Cut cabbage in thick wedges. Sauté meat in butter for five minutes. Add seasonings. Arrange cabbage wedges on meat in skillet. Pour hot water over cabbage. Cover and simmer 20 minutes or until cabbage is tender. Serves six.

PORK AND SAUSAGE

HEAD CHEESE

3 pounds pork meat
3/4 gallon salted water
1 tablespoon lemon juice
1 tablespoon vinegar
3 cups chopped onions
3 cups chopped celery

1 teaspoon bay leaves (powdered)
1 teaspoon sage
1/4 teaspoon mace
1/4 teaspoon red pepper
1 teaspoon black pepper

Boil pork meat (head, feet, tongue, and heart) in 3/4 gallon of salted water with lemon juice and vinegar for 2 hours or until meat falls off bones. Reserve water. Grind, chop or shred meat. Add chopped vegetables that have been lightly sauteed in butter. Add seasonings. Combine meat, vegetables and stock and pour into shallow pans to cool. When it has congealed, slice and serve with crackers.

PORT ROYAL BAKED HAM

6 pound ham
one 8-ounce can crushed pineapple
whole cloves

1 teaspoon cinnamon
1/4 cup molasses

Place ham in baking dish. Cut through skin of ham in crisscross shape one inch apart. Pierce ham with cloves, one clove in each one inch square. Combine pineapple, molasses and cinnamon. Cover ham with pineapple mix. Bake at 300° for one hour basting frequently.

PORK AND SAUSAGE

JOLLY ROGER HAM CASSEROLE

3 cups ham cut into 1 inch cubes
1 chopped bell pepper
6 well scrubbed potatoes cut into 1 inch cubes, skin on
1 chopped onion
1 can cream of mushroom soup

1/2 cup milk
1/2 teaspoon salt
1/4 teaspoon pepper
1/4 teaspoon cayenne pepper
1 cup grated monterey jack cheese

Combine all ingredients in a large bowl. Mix together well. Pour into large casserole and cover. Bake in 325° oven for 50 minutes. Serve with fresh French bread and Creole Cole Slaw. Serves eight.

RAE'S PORK ROAST

4 pound rolled pork roast
1 teaspoon salt
1/4 teaspoon black pepper
1 tablespoon Worcestershire sauce

1 cup water
2 sliced apples
3 cups fresh or frozen brussels sprouts

Heat oven to 350°. Place roast in baking dish. Combine Worcestershire sauce with water. Pour over roast. Sprinkle with salt and pepper. Bake for one hour. Baste with sauce from meat. Add apples and brussels sprouts. Continue cooking one hour more or until meat is done to your liking. Serves eight.

PORK AND SAUSAGE

STUFFED PORK CHOPS

eight 1-inch thick pork chops
1 cup chopped apricots
1/4 cup butter
1 cup chopped onions
3 cups bread crumbs

1 cup seedless raisins
1/4 teaspoon cinnamon
1/2 teaspoon sage
1/4 cup water

Sauté onions in butter. Add apricots, bread crumbs, raisins, cinnamon, sage and water as needed. Insert sharp knife into side of chops and slice open a pocket for stuffing. Fill each chop with stuffing. Secure with tooth picks. Carefully brown on both sides. Place in a large casserole. Bake at 350° for 1 hour. Serves eight.

BUCCANEER TENDERLOIN

2 pounds pork tenderloin

Sauce
1/4 cup molasses
1/2 cup orange juice
1/2 teaspoon salt
1/4 teaspoon black pepper

Slice tenderloin lengthwise into 1" thick pieces. Combine all sauce ingredients. Marinate meat in sauce overnight or at least 4 hours. Drain excess sauce before you BBQ or broil. Use excess sauce to baste during cooking.

PORK AND SAUSAGE

HISPANIOLA HAM SOUFFLÉ

1 teaspoon butter
1 cup minced ham
1/4 cup minced onion
1/4 cup minced celery

4 eggs — separate whites from yolks
1/4 teaspoon cayenne
1/4 teaspoon salt

Sauté ham, onion and celery in butter. Cool. Beat egg whites until fluffy. Combine ham, onion, celery and egg yolks. Beat well. Fold in egg whites. Pour into well-greased casserole dish. Bake 10 minutes at 350°.

PORKERS

2 cups ground sausage
3/4 cup flour
1 teaspoon baking powder
1/3 cup milk

1 large egg
1/2 cup drained, crushed pineapple
1 teaspoon anise seeds
oil for deep frying

Fry sausage and drain off oil. Combine milk, egg, pineapple, anise seeds and cooked sausage. Slowly add flour and baking powder, mixing until well blended. Drop by teaspoons into hot oil (350°). Fry until golden brown. Drain on absorbent paper or old pirate maps.

The Curse of the Corsairs

England wasn't alone when it came to hiring privateers to wreak havoc on enemy vessels. France had its band of hired assassins as well. They became known as the Corsairs. Their base was on a small island near Honduras. Like England, they held a special disdain for the Spanish.

Known for brutality and their small, swift vessels, the Corsairs were a formidable lot. Their macho reputation drew large numbers of recruits mostly made up of deserters and renegade sailors. One of the most notorious was "Peg-leg LeClerc."

Peg-leg led a famous raid on Havana. While holding the city at siege, he kidnapped wealthy citizens and exacted high ransoms. LeClerc relieved the Catholic Church of all its gold and precious jewels. Following a three-week campaign of destruction, Peg-leg and his Corsair army left laden with stolen wealth. Havana was turned into an impoverished and smoldering town with a large cemetery.

As France's holdings grew, so did French piracy. The late 1600's produced yet another Corsair with a flair for brutality, Montbars the Exterminator. He deeply hated the Spanish after they caused the death of his uncle in a ship explosion. Montbars joined the infamous Brothers of the Coast, and with his new brotherhood of desperate characters spent his days ravaging Spanish cities and vessels. His most famous exploit was the attack on the city of Maracaibo where he ruthlessly tortured citizens for weeks to get information on where treasure

was buried. Later he escaped through a Spanish harbor blockade, using a burning ship as a massive inferno torch that enflamed enemy vessels. The Spanish Main faced many threats during the 17th century, but the Corsairs were a primary source of trouble with the likes of Montbars and Peg-leg LeClerc.

PIRATES HALL OF SHAME

Montbars the Exterminator

12: • BEEF
       • GAME

The End of the Terror

The cannons were finally silenced and the last pirate brought to justice and hung around 1830. We know that "all good things must end," but it is reassuring to know that a few bad things do also. Of course, there are still a few today who feel it is their lot in life to carry on the tradition of the desperados, and they will always be with us. At least the organized system of terror which lasted 300 years has unfurled its sails for the last time.

The Blackbeards, William Kidds, Mary Reads and Henry Morgans are but faint echoes from the past. Their muskets blast away no longer and the sound of clanging steel is a distant memory, but the legends of their adventures and exploits still fire the imagination about a time when men (and women) grabbed the wind and sailed into the the history books. The West Indies has never been the same since.

Like a mighty Northeaster that blows in from the calm sea, the reign of the pirates howled furiously, did its damage and then disappeared as mysteriously as it arrived. When a great storm has passed through, all that's left to do is to pick up the pieces and try to put things back together and pray it doesn't happen again. That is what the Caribbean and the Americas have been doing for the past 150 years.

BEEF AND GAME

BOURBON STREET MEAT LOAF

1 1/2 pounds lean ground round
1 1/2 pound cajun sausage (remove casings) hot
 as you like it
1/4 teaspoon black pepper
1/2 teaspoon salt
1 cup chopped onions
1 cup chopped celery
2 minced garlic cloves

2 beaten eggs
1 cup bread or cracker crumbs
1/2 cup broth from can of French Onion soup
Sauce:
 French Onion soup
 2 cups water
 1 tablespoon corn starch

Heat oven to 325°. Mix all ingredients (except for sauce). You might prefer to use your hands to be sure the two meats are well blended. Shape into a loaf or baking pan. Bake 45 minutes. In small sauce pan pour remaining soup, two cups of water and corn starch. Bring to a boil. Cook until thickened. Pour over meat loaf. Continue to bake for 15 minutes more. Serves eight.

GRILLADES AND GRITS

2 pounds lean round steak
1 teaspoon salt
1/2 teaspoon black pepper
1/4 pound sliced bacon

2 tablespoons flour
1 large sliced onion
2 cups stewed tomatoes with juice
1/4 teaspoon cayenne pepper

Cut meat into four to six steaks. Rub salt and pepper into meat. Set aside. Fry bacon in large skillet. Brown steaks on both sides in oil with bacon. Remove meat. Add flour, stirring to brown lightly. Add onions, tomatoes and pepper. Saute for five minutes. Return steaks to skillet. Reduce heat. Cover. Simmer for 45 minutes or until meat is tender. Water should be added as needed to keep a thick gravy at all times in pan. Serve with grits.

BEEF AND GAME

CAJUN POT ROAST

4 pounds lean roast
1 teaspoon salt
1/4 teaspoon pepper
1/2 teaspoon horseradish
2 tablespoons butter

one 8-ounce can spicy V8
6 large potatoes, peeled, quartered
6 large carrots, peeled, halved
2 onions, quartered

Heat oven to 325°. Mix salt, pepper, horseradish and butter together. Spread over roast. Place in roaster or large casserole. Cover and place in oven. Cook for 30 minutes. Add V8 and vegetables. Cover and cook for one hour more or until potatoes are tender. Serves eight.

STEWED SQUIRREL

2 squirrels (use spotted armadillo if squirrels are out of season)
1 cup flour
1/2 teaspoon salt
1/4 teaspoon pepper
1/2 pound sliced bacon cut into pieces
1 cup chopped onion

2 minced garlic cloves
2 bay leaves
1 cup sliced mushrooms
2 cups stewed tomatoes
3 large potatoes cut into 1 inch cubes
2 cups water

Skin and clean squirrels. Cut at joints into serving pieces. Shake pieces in paper bag containing flour, salt and pepper. Fry bacon. Saute onion and garlic with bacon. Add squirrel, browning on all sides. Add bay leaves, mushrooms, tomatoes, potatoes and two cups of water. Simmer over medium heat for one hour or until tender. Serves six.

BEEF AND GAME

CREOLE ROUND STEAK

2-3 pounds lean round steak
2 teaspoons salt
1/2 teaspoon pepper
1/2 teaspoon garlic powder
1 cup flour

1/4 cup oil
2 sliced onions
2 cups canned stewed tomatoes
2 tablespoons Worcestershire sauce
water

Combine salt, pepper, garlic and flour. Sprinkle flour mix over steak and pound well with tenderizer or meat mallet. Turn meat and repeat process until all flour mix is used. Saute onions in oil. Remove onions. Brown steak on both sides. Cover with onions, tomatoes and Worcestershire sauce. Reduce heat to low. Add water to make sauce. Cook for 45 minutes to one hour until tender. Serves eight.

VENISON ROAST

5 pound venison roast
Marinade sauce:
  2 cups vinegar
  1 quart water
  1 tablespoon salt
  2 bay leaves

1 large onion, sliced
2 crushed garlic cloves
1 teaspoon thyme
1 teaspoon oregano
6 strips uncooked bacon

Place roast in large bowl. Mix all ingredients together except bacon and pour over roast. Cover and refrigerate for 12 hours. Heat oven to 300°. Place roast in roasting pan. Cover with bacon strips. Pour two cups of marinade over meat before roasting. Baste every 1/2 hour. Roast for 30 minutes per pound. Time may vary. Check for tenderness.

Patriot or Pirate?

Jean Lafitte

The Lafitte brothers, Jean and Pierre, ran a busy blacksmithing shop on Bourbon Street in New Orleans at the beginning of the 19th century. But that was just their day job. It was really a cover-up business for their real vocation—piracy. Their prime targets were wealthy Spanish galleons and any ship loaded with "Black Ivory," slaves coming from Africa.

They established a slave camp on an island at the mouth of the Mississippi and commanded a band of 2,000 cutthroats to guard their illegal slave trade and terrorize Spanish vessels in the Caribbean. Jean Lafitte's hatred of the Spanish was a deep one. He always blamed them for the suicide of his young bride, and he lived to avenge that death.

It wasn't the Spanish that made Lafitte well known; it was the English. During the War of 1812 they had tried to persuade Jean and his lawless band to help them defeat the Americans in an invasion. Lafitte went instead to the American side and joined Andrew "Stonewall" Jackson. With his desperado militia, LaFitte fought side-by-side with American soldiers in the Battle of New Orleans, giving England one of its worst military defeats. Lafitte instantly became a hero and a patriot.

Did Jean Lafitte live out his life as the great American hero signing autographs and kissing babies? Not exactly. It seems that once the adventure of piracy got into a man's blood, it was hard to get out. Jean moved his base of operations to Galveston Island in Texas and returned to Caribbean waters, robbing everything that moved, including American ships. The US Navy had no option but to put an end to this menace. In 1820, the history portion of the Lafittes ends, and the legends begin. Jean and company, feeling the heat, fled from Galveston with big grins on their faces and ten million dollars in loot in the hold. Off they sailed into the sunset, never to be heard from again.

Rumor has it that they left another ten million buried on Galveston Island just in case they came back. Blacksmith shops weren't cheap, you know.

13 · DESSERTS
· BEVERAGES

DESSERTS

PAT'S PRALINE TEMPTATIONS

2 cups packed dark brown sugar
2 cups white sugar
1 12 ounce can evaporated milk
1/2 cup butter

1/4 teaspoon salt
1 teaspoon vanilla
2 cups pecans

In a large skillet combine sugars, milk, butter and salt. Cook over medium heat, stirring frequently to soft ball stage (236°, small amount of mixture dropped in cold water forms a soft ball). Remove from heat and add vanilla and pecans. Drop by large spoonfuls onto greased cookie sheet. Cool before serving.

ORILLES DE COCHEN (PIGS EARS)

2 cups flour
2 teaspoons baking powder
1/2 teaspoon salt
2 beaten eggs

1/2 cup melted butter
enough oil to deep fry
1 cup pure cane syrup
1 cup finely chopped nuts

Heat oil in deep skillet to 350°. Combine flour, baking powder and salt. Add beaten eggs to melted, cooled butter then add to flour mix, blending well. Divide into 16 balls. Roll each ball to an eight inch, thin, round pastry. Drop into hot oil twisting in center with fork to form the shape of a pigs ear. When golden brown, remove from oil and drain on absorbent paper. Drizzle with hot syrup and sprinkle with chopped nuts.

DESSERTS

BELT POPPIN' PECAN PIE

1 unbaked 9 inch pie shell
1/2 cup dark brown sugar
1 cup corn syrup
3 eggs well beaten

3 tablespoons butter
1 teaspoon vanilla
1 cup pecans

Heat oven to 325°. In a large bowl combine sugar, syrup, eggs, butter and vanilla, whipping vigorously all the time. Fold in pecans. Pour into pie shell. Bake for 35 minutes.

BLACKBEARD'S GRUEL

2 cups cooked rice
1 1/2 cups milk
pinch of salt
1 teaspoon vanilla
1/4 teaspoon cinnamon

1/4 teaspoon nutmeg
1/2 cup brown sugar
1/2 cup raisins
3 eggs beaten until fluffy

Preheat oven to 300°. Gently fold all ingredients together adding fluffy eggs last. Pour into well-greased baking dish. Bake 30 minutes. Serve hot or cold. Serves six.

DESSERTS

LADY MICHELLE'S FRUIT CRUSH

Fresh, frozen or canned fruit can be used
1 cup strawberries (for pink color), or
1 cup peeled kiwi (for green color)
1 cup skinned peaches

1 peeled banana
1 cup orange juice
2 cups ice cubes

Place orange juice and ice cubes in blender. Run on high until smooth. Turn off and add fruit. Blend until smooth. Pour into glasses. Garnish with mint leaves.

BEIGNETS

3/4 cup water
3/4 cup flour
1/4 cup butter
8 well beaten eggs

1 teaspoon vanilla
1/2 teaspoon ground cardamom
1 cup confectioners sugar
oil for deep frying

Combine water, flour and butter in sauce pan. Bring to boil, stirring constantly. Remove from heat. Add Vanilla, cardamom and slowly add beaten eggs, mixing thoroughly and briskly. Heat oil to 350°. Drop batter by large tablespoonfuls into oil. Fry until golden on all sides. Drain on absorbent paper and dust with confectioners sugar.

DESSERTS

PECAN COCONUT MACAROONS

3 cups shredded coconut
1 cup chopped pecans

one 14-ounce can sweetened condensed milk
1 teaspoon vanilla

Mix all ingredients. Drop by spoonfuls on greased baking sheet. Bake at 350° for approximately five minutes. Do not burn. Cool before serving. Makes four dozen.

ROYAL BOUNTY BREAKFAST COOKIES

3/4 cup sugar
3/4 cup butter
2 eggs
1/2 teaspoon ground cardamom

2 cups flour
1 teaspoon baking powder
1/4 teaspoon salt

Cream butter, sugar and eggs. Combine flour, baking powder, cardamom and salt. Add flour mix to butter/sugar mix. Shape dough into balls using 1 tablespoon dough for each cookie. Bake on cookie sheets in 350° oven for 10 minutes.

CAFE AU LAIT

2 cups milk
1/4 cup sugar

4 cups coffee

Bring milk almost to a boil. Add sugar then add to very hot fresh brewed coffee.

DESSERTS

CHOCOLATE SPONGE CAKE

3/4 cup flour
1/4 teaspoon salt
1/4 cup cocoa
5 egg yolks

1 teaspoon vanilla
5 egg whites
1 cup sugar

Mix flour, salt and cocoa together. Beat egg yolks together with vanilla. Beat egg whites until they are stiff and peaked. Fold in egg yolks, a small amount at a time. Fold in flour mixture, a small amount at a time. Bake in an ungreased tube pan for 1 hour at 325°.

COFFEE BLIZZARD

2 cups cold coffee
1 cup cold milk

1 cup French vanilla ice cream
1 cup ice cubes

Place coffee and milk in blender. Add ice cubes. Blend on high until ice is completely crushed. Turn blender speed down and add ice cream. Blend until smooth. Top with whipped cream and sprinkle with cinnamon. Serve immediately.

The Man Who Buried His Bible

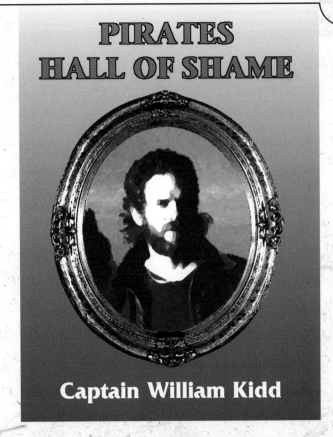

Captain William Kidd

Privateering had been good to Captain William Kidd. He had defended England's honor in the Caribbean. A well-earned hero status was his to enjoy. Wealth was also his to enjoy, and that is what he did. His real estate holdings in New York were substantial, and he had settled into the domestic life of a wealthy merchant with a wife and children. If he had only stopped there! But the call of adventure and great riches on the high seas was too strong and he decided to go on just one more privateering mission.

The voyage turned out to be a grinding, unprofitable one. The angry crew grew restless and threatened mutiny. In an argument, Captain Kidd slammed a wooden bucket into a crewman's head and killed him. The restless expedition turned to piracy, and no mercy was shown on any ship that crossed their path. The voyage had become desperate. In a deliberate act of defiance against his Creator, Captain Kidd buried his Bible because it condemned his wicked way of life. But things only went from bad to very bad.

In Madagascar, his crew deserted him and stripped all the guns off the ship. Remarkably, Kidd was able to commandeer a new vessel and convince a crew to sail with him. He returned to New York, stopping only to bury a large amount of treasure in Long Island—a little undeclared income tucked away for retirement. It was an income neither he nor anyone else to this day has seen.

The stories of his exploits preceded him to port where he was convicted of murder and piracy.

When they took him to the gallows, the door mechanism failed to work, so he got a one-day reprieve prolonging his misery until he was hung the next day. One wonders what went through his mind in that final dark day. He probably was trying to remember where he buried that Bible.

ACKNOWLEDGEMENTS

Special appreciation is extended to the 19th century
engravers and painters, whose talent has graced
this book or inspired new art work.

To Sylvia, for her encouragement and editorial work
on the manuscript.

To Bert, for the right suggestions at the right time.

To Janet, for her painstaking research on the recipes
and for 26 wonderful years that makes the author
happy he isn't sailing the Seven Seas.

To Dad, Gary, Mike, Dave, Claude, Nelson, Don and
Cookie for generously providing portraits of the
worst rogues to plunder the Spanish Main.

To God, the Captain and Navigator of our family ship.

Ordering Information

INSTRUCTIONS

Copies of this book may be ordered by using our 800-number service or by mailing in your personal check or money order to the address listed on the order form. Please feel free to photocopy this page to place your order.

All orders received will be shipped promptly, normally within 48 hours of receipt of your payment.

If you are not completely satisfied with your copy of Caribbean Adventures we will refund your money. At Adlai House Publishing we are very concerned that you, our customers, are treated fairly.

ORDER NOW! 1-800-338-6072
Distributed by SHIP TO SHORE, INC.
10500 Mount Holly Rd., Charlotte, N.C. 28214-9219

ORDER DIRECT FROM THE PUBLISHER

· Fill in the enclosed order form.
· Enclose a personal check or money order made out to Adlai House Publishing.
· Mail payment to:

> Adlai House Publishing
> P.O. Box 935
> Lakeside, CA 92040

Caribbean Adventures Order Form

QTY		TOTAL
	X $11.95 each book	
Add Shipping and Handling		$2.00
CA orders – add 7% tax ($.83)		
TOTAL ENCLOSED		

Mail payment to :
> Adlai House Publishing
> P.O. Box 935
> Lakeside, CA 92040

You may photocopy this page